How to Start Your Own
Secret Society

Oldcastle Books

Other titles from the same author

How to Start Your Own Secret Society

Nick Harding

Oldcastle Books

This edition first published in 2006 by Oldcastle Books,
Harpenden, Herts, UK

@OldcastleBooks
oldcastlebooks.co.uk

A CIP catalogue record for this book is available from the British Library.

ISBN 10: 1 904048 84 6
ISBN 13: 978 1 904048 84 8

2 4 6 8 10 9 7 5 3

Typeset by Avocet Typeset, Bideford, Devon, EX39 2BP
Printed and bound in Great Britain by CPI Group (UK) Ltd, Croydon CR0 4YY

For Andrea
La mia piccola pesca

Voluminous thanks to the usual crowd of beer soaked
reprobates I call my chums.
My family for their love and support.
Sir Francis Dashwood.
Richard Dawkins and Carl Sagan.
My agent Annabel Nash for having to put up with the
incessant tidal wave of scrawled manuscripts.
And
To secret societies everywhere.

May Leonardo Da Vinci's reputation be returned
to its rightful status...

A lifetime of thanks to Bros. Calvert, Martin, Kaye, Stansfield,
Lightfoot, Whydle, Saunders, Harding and Richards of *The
Regency*, *Crown* and *The Queens* Lodges for their support. Bro.
Morton of Lodges *Kilbryde* and *Shalom*. And to the BEC for their
continued underground activities.

A version of the article on wigs, secret societies and caving first
appeared in the *Belfry Bulletin* – Journal of the Bristol
Exploration Club (not a secret society), Summer 2005 Vol. 54,
No 2. Number 522.

Contents

CONTENTS

CONTENTS

Introduction

Nam et ipsa scientia potestas est...
(Knowledge itself is power)

Bacon, *Religious Meditations, of Heresies.*

Procul, o procul este, profani.
(Far, far from me, let all profane ones be)

Virgil, *Aeneid*

Welcome to the heady and exciting world of secret societies. From ancient times to the present man, and it is predominantly a male preoccupation, has sought to shut himself away in tight unapproachable enclaves with like-minded individuals. Protected by the walls of a lodge, he revels in the company of others, plotting the downfall of western civilisation, governments and the Church or constructing methods of world domination. He has concocted elaborate rituals for the purposes of self-gratification or the swearing of solemn vows of adherence to convince acolytes that they are party to something special. He has carefully worked out subtle signs and symbols of recognition so that fellow members can identify each other in a wide variety of social functions, business trans-

11

actions and legal arenas. And he has sworn loyalty and fraternal fellowship to his brotherhood on pain of death should his loyalty falter or he reveal the secrets contained therein.

Whatever the average man in the street's opinions, thoughts and views on the machinations of secret societies, whether substantiated or not, many are desperate to join, believing that this sought after membership will aid them to fortune, favour and a better social standing. They offer a sense of security in a very insecure world. Humanity is at its heart a tribal species and has a tendency to congregate thus for mutual support.

Of course many are turned away because they do not meet the specified requirements, the social gravitas or influence to join. Many, who join, or rather are asked to join, are already known figures in the local community – a person with the ability to make things happen. A man of position. A man of power. Some are colleagues and associates of those already enshrined within an order. Some enter a secret society by birth.

Many are desperate to join but they have, perhaps in the past, somehow sullied their reputations and copybooks or more likely, and this is often the case, their 'faces do not fit'. A denigrating and mis-timed remark about an acquaintance's car, golf handicap or earning capacity may have the later knock-on effect of barring that person from membership of a secret society: they have been, to use the vernacular term, '*black-balled*'. Most secret societies prefer people of a certain social standing, offering those elements that display low moral fibre and a slack work ethic within the population at large no access to such an institution. A man of means is of value to others within the order. An individual with ample coinage has the ability to bail another out of a bad situation. A secret society that is poor in wealth as well as morality will not last long.

Fear not! None of this should be a hindrance or a stigma. To that person constantly rejected by Freemasonry, the Hellfire Club, the Rosicrucians, the Knights Templar and is not part of the Old Boy/School Tie network, this book is a balm for their troubled soul.

This guide illustrates the generic requirements needed to set up and run a secret society. By doing this the constantly rejected enthusiast can do away with petitioning or brown nosing in favour of a deep sense of self worth, social standing of his or her own making and the comforting knowledge that they are party to hidden arcana known only to themselves and their lodge members. A wonderful concept in itself. You can create a tough, energetic organisation with a hard-nosed outlook and a desire to run the world or you can develop a more gentler, light hearted cabal, akin perhaps to the *Calves' Head Club* who took the mickey out of Charles I with food dolled up in fancy dress.

This book will describe (among other things) the secrets needed, the rituals required, logos and badges, recognition signals, what to wear, initiation ceremonies (including who can join), who should be Grand Master, agendas (spiritual enlightenment versus earthly matters such as politics), gaining influence (at the local or international level), increasing membership and turning away those who don't measure up. It also highlights the methods for developing a reputation and the arguments on whether to stay secret or not, along with the processes employed to put the wind up the general public, the Church and conspiracy theorists in equal measure – usually of course by doing absolutely nothing.

I

In Which the Basics are Discussed

Behold, I tell you a mystery;
we shall not all sleep,
but we shall all be changed.

1 Corinthians 15:51

Fundamentals

Fill, fill, to the brim,
Freely drink and cheerly sing,
Long life and luck to him,
Who does the apron wear.

Mathew Garland (1742–1819) of Deptford,
Worshipful Master, Masonic poet and auctioneer

So you have decided to start a secret society. An excellent endeavour! By doing so you have stepped upon a path of a lifelong commitment to upholding those values you find dear. By enshrining those tenets in a hidden conclave you will strengthen their attributes and improve your social status, to the point where you will admonish those who have constantly run you down or done you great disservice in the past. You will, of course, find yourself in the company of like-minded individuals all of whom share your desires, beliefs and points of view. In this modern world with its nefarious uncertainties there is nothing more satisfying and, indeed, comforting, in a non-threatening or overtly sexual manner, to find others of similar outlook. One seeks the warmth of the bonds of friendship, loyalty and protection in the safe redoubt that only a secret society can bring. In times of desperate need there is solace in the knowledge that there are others who will come to your aid. There is nothing more dutiful or indeed honorable to be found in any social milieu than that.

With this honorable duty and solemn vow I cross from the realm of isolation to the brotherhood of protection. May I find a lodge when needed and may I be that which others, who may seek me out, when they are in their nadir, require.

Loftus Bathe-Tydering,
'*A Man Must Be a Lodge*',

from *Toasts From the Top Table:
An Anthology of Secret Society Secrets* (1805)

Origins

First things first. Secret societies have existed throughout human history and probably started in the earliest cultures as a ritualised process by which the transition from child to man, a crossing of a threshold into adulthood, could be easily facilitated. This is still seen today in numerous tribal and religious groups throughout the world. Men also possessed the tendency to separate themselves into male only 'lodges' in which certain skills were honed, such as those of hunting, drinking or having a damn good moan about the next tribe. This would have progressed and developed into what was known as the 'priestly caste' (in Egypt, Greece, Rome) – those individuals who considered themselves the only ones who were capable of communing with the gods. Subsequently these spiritual divisions would have splintered into groups,

who had, perhaps, different ideas about their belief systems –
maybe even having heretical ideas from the prevailing ideologies and therefore needing the protection of secrecy. Into this
mix would have been the earliest blacksmiths – with their
'otherworldly' knowledge about metalworking, followed by
healers and wise folk – such as the witches who, because of
their secret knowledge and therefore special status, lived their
lives on the edge of communities.

Some, predominantly later secret societies, were set up,
usually by wealthy philanthropists, for benevolent and charitable reasons. They shifted emphasis to assist the poor and
the sick, surrendering their apparent clandestine activities to
perform purely altruistic acts of heartfelt compassion.

There is a basic tendency in human culture towards an
elitist separation (perhaps the most obvious trait any secret
society can possess) whether it is in the male-only world of
Turkish chefs where women are forbidden from the kitchens
to the Knights of Malta, the only organisation without a
country who have special observer status at the UN, and on
through to the fraternity houses of American colleges. In
many respects it would be more surprising if secret societies
did not exist, such is the nature of 'tribal man'.

Anyway, setting one up can be a rich (psychologically, as
well as financially) and rewarding experience. It can give
you hours of pleasure as well as advanced social standing and
an influence you always thought was far beyond your reach.

Caveat: You will also become the centre of unwarranted
attention from those who will display nothing but a vehe-
ment antagonism towards your newly founded cadre (Bad
luck!). Pay them no heed. As with most things in life allow
jealousy to sway others, not yourself. Besides, you will have

more important things to worry about, such as regalia or rituals. Do not hinder the setting up of your society through fear of what others may think. Let them believe what they like – they will anyway, whatever you say or do. Throughout history members of secret societies have been vilified, demonised, castigated, trounced upon and generally victimized, simply for not following society's so called norms, even those with charitable outlooks. If this happens to you then take comfort in the fact that you are not alone and are part of a long and proud tradition of standing up to the 'throwers of fruit'.

He was the very Devil sporting his rear through the streets of the village like a wanton imp and as we feared he was a duplicitous and ignoble member of that which we desired to see fall. He had knowledge of Devillysh thyngs, which required the Reverend to chastise him and the lodge he belonged unto. I ordered that the populace thus launch broadsides of rotted fruit at the man for he was deserved of such for his membership of a Satanic cult such as his.

Hinton Blewitt,
Mayor of Ubley
Letters From the Narrow Minded,
Collected 1768

You must take comfort in the fact that you will be surrounded by the people who matter, specifically your loyal companions, and should you fall under 'satiric observation' you must realise that outsiders are looking upon you out of a burning jealous desire to know exactly what it is you are being secretive about. As is always the case they will fear what they do not know. In short, be prepared for trouble but solid support close at hand will facilitate an easy weathering of any storm.

In my need of troubled woes I found myself lucky to be in the company of men who had been themselves rejected by the indifferent world and being a man of such impecuniousness I was facilitated an easy recovery from such financial maladies by the generosity of gentlemen who saw fit to assist in my return to grace.

But I was duly outcast from my gentleman's club and assisted from certain other interests because I engaged in fraternising with fellowes named the Ordines who were looked upon with such ravages of malodorous and satiric observation that I could scarce shew my face upon the hours of daylight less men of the parish set about me with sticks and batons.

But I worried not for I was with stout company who were better than blood relatives in their administrations of protection and I soon found the company of such brothers superior to that one may encounter in any institution abroad in this land. In essence I cared not for the opinions of others for I had rejected the world of the profane and had stepped upon the path to fraternal understanding.

Gideon Mantell,
15th Grand Master of the Ordines
Extract from the *Diary of an Accepted Outcast*,
Folio 1757

Gideon Mantell was the most successful Grand Master of the Ordines, a secret society set up not long after the Renaissance to protect scientific knowledge from '*certaine forces*'. Despite his rejection by the population of the every day world, who looked upon him with a great deal of enraged suspicion he made the Ordines the force it is today. Through his diligence the Ordines were able to survive the acts of parliament of 1799 banning secret societies, a rabid fever that was born out the wild conspiracies drummed up by numerous written works including Robison's 1797 book, *Proof of a Conspiracy*, which was aimed at Freemasonry. In his book Robison accused Freemasonry of trying to subvert government and religion through a symbolic based conspiracy. But like most extreme ideas it proved to be groundless. It is interesting to note that in recent years, world-shattering events such as the Kennedy Assassination and the attacks on the World Trade Center have also been blamed on Freemasons, particularly from the more outré and deliriously paranoid sections of the community. Like the Freemasons have done, pay these delusions no heed.

Care not for those beyond the door, they offer little but persecution and will mock your certainties. It is not to say that they are beyond redemption but you should concern yourself with thine own matters only. Master thyself and not the world. One is possible; the other an up hill task beyond even the fortitude of the gods. And even they have given up.

Thomas Glabb
Concerning Lodge Matters,
Slough 1776

Sir Francis Dashwood (more on him later) was branded a Satanist after rumours and virulent propaganda were spread about his Hellfire Club, the last of several fraternal associations he had devised, which he set up in the mid 1700s to howls of great criticism. In essence Dashwood chose to follow the ideals of Dionysian carousing and having a jolly good time. Jealous puritanical and overtly religious individuals, annoyed that someone was actually enjoying themselves, set about the man branding him, in no uncertain terms, a dangerous subversive. Even 250-odd years ago, as it is today, there were people in this country trying to stop individuals supping at the fountain of life by sullying the reputation of a secret society.

On the Other Hand

At the opposite end of the spectrum you must also be prepared for the inevitable interest that you will acquire the moment you suggest to friends in the nook, over foaming pints of ale, that you are about to embark on the thrilling and fulfilling activity of creating a secret society. Doubtless there will be a period of humorous leg pulling, even some creative suggestions in opposition to the negative, but if you are determined and strong willed you will soon discover that those around you will be fully supportive of your goal – especially if promises of early membership swiftly ensue. Again, be circumspect in discussing too many issues at this stage, particularly in terms of 'secrets'. If too many people know what these are before you are underway it will dilute the initiation process and power of your group. Certainly this bridge will have to be crossed eventually, but not too soon. Allow a healthy period of gestation to occur. Be open to suggestions, but only discuss such matters with trustworthy associates.

It is often wise, having begun the initial stages, to develop a back-up strategy. Should the trust be broken between you and your colleagues – perhaps the secret society is discussed too often in public places – whether as part of a deliberate policy to 'spoil the show' or through simple carelessness, having policies known only to yourself will be of great benefit. If you have developed fallback procedures you may incorporate them later on as 'higher degree knowledge', and then nothing is wasted.

Having told him of my desire to embellish my life with something beyond the norm, I inquired as to his strategy in the formation and construction of his Brotherhood. His rejoinder, quick on the heels of my question was a brusque hand gesture and the words; 'it shall not be discussed…'

Josiah Stang
Conversations with a Lush, 1856

What Kind of Society?

Probably the most important question you will be asked is: '*What kind of secret society are you forming?*' Well, in answer you must be circumspect, particularly in the early months of its genesis. This is not to supply secrecy or premature gravitas, although it certainly helps, but as a way to allow yourself time to consider what class of secret society you are going to develop. Is it going to be political or esoteric? Will you have plans for world domination? Subverting legal or financial institutions? Will you be a benevolent charity keen to help your fellow man or will you concentrate on more malevolent ideals such as Satanism or pornographic frivolity? Will you simply carouse or will you attempt to enlighten the world around you? Will you enjoy the pleasures of the cup or the search for the Holy Grail? (After deciding, of course, what exactly that is.) Will you protect some (copyrighted) secret or attempt to rewrite history through the use of crude literature? These decisions may also have some influence on what you call your secret society. But do not rush. A name is just as important as what you do. Care is needed.

No subject is too extreme or indeed too simple to use as a starting point. The following example highlights the idea that even the most innocent of occupations, in this case wig making, is not beyond careful consideration. The extract below is taken from *The History of Secret Societies in Somerset* by Hampton Peabody, who was himself a member of the Ancient Order of the Ring Slippy Tweed, a now defunct secret society who revelled, it is said, in nude caving. As you will see caving, wigs and secret societies are blended together in a fascinating ensemble.

'In the early days of cave exploration the development of special forms of wig became a staple of any subterranean investigator's equipment. Limited as that burgeoning kit was; a few candles, muslin bags of boiled sweets, and a sturdy pair of pantaloons, the cave wig became essential dress for the gentleman explorer.

The Bath wig makers Mssrs Absolom and Loftus Racketts of Protozoan Road became the cavers' emporium of choice. Within its wainscoted boudoirs a voluminous collection of assorted caving paraphernalia could be found, albeit mostly of the false hair variety. From this same establishment members of the various secret societies in the area could attend to their lodge wardrobe without fear of discovery. The premises also doubled as a lodge for the *Wigboys* – a fraternal brotherhood set up to promote the use of false headwear. During a coffee shop debacle in which numerous drinks were spilt the brotherhood was forced underground to avoid the attentions of the law.

It is known that local cave aficionado Dr Catcott (himself a Ring Slippy Tweedian) often frequented the shop on his way to swap tales of derring-do with other local men of an exploratory nature in the region's coffee-houses and Masonic lodges. Catcott himself preferred the Dorset Fancy for walks but opted for the heavier, indeed sturdier Pentland Thunderer (not to be confused with the whistle of the same name) for subterranean activities. With its thicker inner weave it afforded a certain higher level of protection than the Frobisher Light, a wig often used for inspecting holes in the Mendip region, and was also the headgear of choice for the Bed Fellows, a gentlemen-only cadre who indulged in prolonged bouts of lying around. For at least two generations the Frobisher had been de rigueur in Somerset for men out inspecting cavities, natural or suspiciously man made alike. Its blend of horsehair, weasel and Haart's Wildebeest allowed the wearer to keep his head warm and reasonably waterproof in a brisk squall. But, as the user's manual suggested in the most adamant of terms, the wearer should seek shelter at the first opportunity. A side effect of a sudden downpour was to shrink the wig to embarrassing dimensions, forcing the owner, unless he himself was lacking in the hair department, into offering the headgear to friends and fellows with less atop. In many respects and at that stage it mirrored the 'scratch wig'; one whose sole purpose was to cover bald spots.

A similar side effect could be seen with the 'Dorset Fancy', a light summer wig mostly used for those seeking Marsh fritillaries, and indeed other members of the lepidotera family, for their gentlemen's collections. The wig itself was even issued with its own collecting jar while the hair piece itself, due to its gossamer construction, was delicate enough to be used for catching all kinds of ephemeral insects. Because of its lightness it could easily be forgotten by the wearer that he was sporting such apparel. As the Hon. Sir Hugh Bending-Slow (A Grand Master of The Cheddar Rattlers) wrote in his *The Wig,*

*It's Uses, Non-Uses and General Abuse of Said Hairpiece
Usually in the Manner of Whipping Servants, Book Four.*

> *"It beist unseemly for a man to wear his Dorset Fancy for
> anything other than the most convivial of summer excur-
> sions. It beist a moral outrage and Devilish invidious
> behaviour if said headular investment be espied on evening
> occasions."*

It was not uncommon for ladies to swoon and or duels
to be fought over such insidious social faux pas, the results
of which were that many a cobbled street beyond the
doors of inns, taverns and lodges were littered with tram-
pled and crumpled insubstantial head adornments, the fall
out, in a manner of speaking, of bellicose activities. The
Dorset Fancy thus assisted (some say was the sole contrib-
utor, see Albert Lamellibranch's *The Revolutionary Wigs of
Britain*) the illegal wig trade that was common throughout
the period, producing such fabled characters, later
members of the *Knights Tonsure*, as Dave the Wigger,
Headpiece Jack, or Wigboy John, gentlemen of the
shadows who would lurk in side alleys until enough
battered wigs had collected on the streets. They would
then spend the following hours collecting as many of the
fallen items as darkness would allow. It was also around this
time that Burke and Hair became famous for digging up
the corpses of unsuspecting members of the aristocracy
and relieving them of their head wear and Masonic regalia.
The recently freed hairpieces were hastily smuggled to the
backrooms of numerous rival wig-making facilities so that
their intricate weaves could be studied and analysed. This

'*regalia*' was often sold on to dubious market traders keen to infiltrate the lodges of the county for personal gain.

It was not until the introduction of the 'Devon Loafa' that certain characters interested in underground activities, other than those of a revolutionary nature, realised they could push further into the recesses of dark vaults as a direct result of the sturdy weave of the new kid on the head block. The Loafa had a thicker, more voluminous appearance and had been created by Abraham Snapcock, whose shop was situated near the Inns of Court in London. From his premises he had observed that judges and their kind had taken to a peculiar sport, one that "*took the form of fancy and elaborate gesticulations and head butting*" (from Chapter 874 of *Snapcock's Diary*). He had initially mistaken these peculiar activities as the recognition rituals of a new secret society but having seen heavy wagers laid down on the cobbles he cottoned on to the fact that it was more a series of sporting events and had nothing to do, at least superficially, with the clandestine machinations of some back room anti-Catholic movement. (Later evidence bore out Snapcock's suspicions when one of his wigs turned up at a wine and cheese party for a book launch.)

With an almost limitless number of wigs on sale none were sturdy enough to support such "*uncivil behaviour*" so Snapcock decided to remedy the situation. After several minutes study he produced the test version of the wig that would eventually evolve into the Thunderer. At this stage it was simply called Old Heavy until it was christened the Devon Loafa by an itinerant Vicar from Barnstaple who narrowly escaped death when a weather vane "*struck me rudely about the head as if a vagabond were attempting to rummage in my vestments,*" and missed braining the man of the cloth by a whisker.

With caving not a pursuit to be seen in and around the streets of the capital the heavier wigs were adopted by those pursuing criminals. Footpads, cutpurses and those with equally low moral fibre often fell victim to a well-aimed wig launched from the hand of a practised member of the King's militia. During the Riot of Idioblastic Street many a miscreant Londoner and secret revolutionary was brought to book with the use of a "*fair volley of head pieces thusly followed by explosive detonations of wig powder that besmirched the walls of the parish*". (Quoted in Lamellibranch's *The Revolutionary Wigs of Britain*, Chapter 2).

William Eggy-Belch, a gentleman from Wells and ardent Cheddar Rattler, was a frequent visitor to London and on one such journey fell unceremoniously into Snapcock's wig merchants after one too many libations in the Gasometer Arms, a few doors down from the purveyor of flamboyant head gear. This in itself was a fortuitous happenstance because Eggy-Belch had earlier that day suffered at the hands of some jobbing actors who had ruffled his 'Boston Hose Pipe' in a badly executed rendition of Samuel Johnson's *The Metamorphic Aureole*. In need of a new wig Eggy-Belch had somehow found himself in the right place at roughly the right time.

Snapcock ushered his wig boy out into the storeroom to retrieve the latest fashions, one of which being of course, the Devon Loafa. Eggy-Belch took to the item with "*unreserved and unashamed gusto!*" He promptly bought eight on the spot.

'Returning to Somerset, Eggy-Belch handed out five of the wigs to his estate labourers who often complained of thick headaches after long sessions repairing the roof beams of sheds and barns. Headaches due in part to the "*lack of a well sought ability in these rude mechanicals to avoid falling timbers thus loosed from the rafters of the buildings I had sent them to repair*". (Isaiah Tittee, *Memoirs of a Somerset Git*, 1848).

It was in the Bulbous Whim, a now demolished Inn in Tucker Street, Wells, the site of which is interestingly enough now occupied by a purveyor of caving and camping equipment, that Eggy-Belch fell into derisory conversation with one Dr Catcott who was hobbling around the city after an unceremonious accident caused by a vigorous bout of country dancing in the parlour of his lodgings while entertaining fellow members of the Ring Slippy Tweedians. Catcott was abroad in the area investigating various orifices, cavities and caverns in the Mendip Hills for a book he was writing called *I Like Holes*. The Bristol Reverend was also having unending trouble with his own wig which, as he said, "...*afforded me no comfort in any shape or form, being troublesome and nefarious to the point that I assumed it to be possessed by one of Satan's noisome imps.*" The Dorset Fancy was soon to be cast aside by the wandering scholar in favour of the Devon Loafa, a welcome gift from Eggy-Belch.

Back in Bristol Catcott had the Loafa further enhanced by his favourite wig merchants, Jonah Deleterious and Sons (a site now occupied by a waste bin in Broadmead), who set about tightening up the weave and adding additional layers to the hair to give it extra protection. There was also a retractable thick wire pin on which a candle could be mounted allowing the explorer hands free illumination while the whole hair-piece itself was coated in a velveteen lacquer to keep it from *"becoming bedecked with ferrous soils and fudgy particulates"*. The ochrous wig was now a thing of the past. The Loafa had become the Thunderer and it would be this overdeveloped wig that would take Catcott into the heart of the Mendips. It would also be the headgear of choice within numerous secret societies in the county; not least the Ring Slippy Tweedians who on Catcott's insistence adopted the hair piece as part of their regalia.'

In all respects it is down to personal taste as to what source is chosen as a prime mover and basis for your secret society. You could take a leaf out of religion's book where dissatisfaction with the prevailing ideology often promotes a splinter group to slough off from the main church. The history of all major religions is replete with numerous examples of such 'budding' in which charismatic individuals feel that either the prevailing belief systems are not fundamental enough or are just too strict.

This also occurs in politics, another major source for secret societies. It has been claimed that culottes sporting proletarian Freemasons were behind the French Revolution, but do not be tempted to read too much into the role of secret societies in the political arena. More often than not a revolution may simply be the result of the desires for social change of a population sick of living off dead rats and street effluvia. The Bastille was full of the middle classes, anyway. Yet this should never stop you. Of course, associating yourself with one colour in the political spectrum will instantly bring you criticism from another. Be aware that vote rigging, election scams and bribery appear in the quiver of skills of any Machiavellian expert in political subterfuge, but they are not necessarily those a secret society should employ. That, though, is entirely up to you. Hoist your political flag and follow its creed. Political expediency is on the whole the purview of specialist para-military or police forces who will probably frown somewhat if you tread on their territorial toes. Be sensitive to their wishes when you can.

If perhaps your politics are to the left of centre you may perceive the world to be heading into some fascistic nightmare. From this fear of domination you may favour a secret society whose main purpose is to resist through the employment of various revolutionary and indeed anarchic methods. The same of course if you fear the opposite – that an extreme left totalitarianism is threatening to turn everyone into mindless, share everything zombies.

You may wish to advance the idea of Atheism in the face of a growing lurch to a new Dark Age or you may desire less secularism and more faith in an attempt to bring about that new Dark Age. Think about what it is that really drives you and use that as your source.

The most important and overriding point to be fully aware of is that the whole process will be a real life-changing event. It will be without question something of a new start, a resurrection, a turning point, and a breath of fresh air to an otherwise (possibly) stale and bland existence. The setting up of a fraternal brother or sisterhood will take over your life to the point where it supersedes any notion of being a hobby, pastime or simple interest.

Once hooked I was unable to rid myself of this glorious distraction from the beige existence that my life had become. I was liberated and reborn into something that was beyond criticism. I was it and it was me...

Neville Quaintly
Macramé, My Life in Threads, 1975

Developing Some History

It may be wise, after you have decided on the form of your secret society, to generate some *back-story* – a term borrowed from the writing and acting professions. This is one of the best ways to add great weight to your ambitions. History brings gravitas, acceptance and in many cases a good deal of revenue. Remember of course that history is written by the victors and is often heavily skewed for propaganda purposes. It is very difficult to sift fact from fiction and personal bias is prevalent even in the reporting of modern events, so to decide what the truth was, say 2,000 years ago can be a real challenge. This, though, has never stopped anyone using history for his or her own gain. Even fake history has its uses.

> *One of the saddest lessons of history is this:*
> *If we've been bamboozled long enough, we*
> *tend to reject any evidence of the bamboozle...*

Carl Sagan
The Demon Haunted World

Perhaps you were once a member of an extant secret society but were hacked off by their approach to things. A clever trick is to appropriate some of their history but remember to adapt it. Simple theft from a rival group will only encourage ire on their behalf and although rivalry will occur, you want that to develop over a period of time and not from the off. As we know beginnings are a delicate time. But fear not. In terms of legality you have to remember that all secret societies claim great heritage over a protracted period of time, in some cases, millennia. Like branches from a tree secret societies blossom and spread in a continuing evolution of the esoteric. It is unlikely that any cadre will want to sue you if you appropriate an idea, as this will leave them open to criticism and legal vulnerability. Very few secret societies are desirous of bad publicity or indeed, a stupendous amount of attention. It tends to nullify the mystique. When that happens, institutions like the Women's Institute beckon. (Contrary to the mad ravings of conspiracy theorists the WI have no desire to control the world through the prestigious use of malicious mind control techniques, plum conserves or knitting. Nor should their voluminous hats be considered as 'regalia'. Keep up the good work ladies! In May 2006 a bugging device was found in the WI hall in Malham, UK – so maybe someone knows differently!)

A useful and clever trick is to tie your back-story into genuine historic events. By performing this feat of grand legerdemain criticism of your organisation will be greatly softened. Who is to say that your secret society was not involved in the setting up of the League of Nations, or that the perennially fun loving and bedroom philosopher Marquis De Sade, before he was sectioned, was not a Grand Master of your happy band of brothers? Who is to say the original members of your brotherhood were not fiddling the troop numbers at the Battle of Austerlitz or tinkering with the cannons at Valley Forge? (Not to be confused with the shame brought upon the Maundy Knights who were caught spiking the Canons at a Preceptory in Amiens.)

Of course be careful not to use the same historic events pertaining to a rival organisation, as this will add not only to some confusion but also to a general dismissal of your claims. And, frankly, who wants that?

I had asked upon the nature of his involvement in the incident at the campaign of Wavering Down but I knew him to be a fibber of the first degree*, for it was my very own brotherhood that had brought about the change in the umpire's decision.

> Hugh Muche-Fudge
> 1st Baron of Cross
> *The Freemasons and Cricket,*
> *Umpires in the Brotherhood Exposed*, 1934

Unfortunately of late, the big historical situations have all been snapped up and heavily copyrighted. Avoid, where you can, tying your society's history into such events as mysterious Papal deaths, the Crucifixion, the assassinations of JFK and RFK, the Cod Wars, the M25, the birth of the United States, the moon landings, the death of Mozart, Atlantis, the National Trust, the Sphinx, introduction of E numbers, celebrity Renaissance inventors and artists, the selling of shell suits, Iraq Invasion #2, the sinking of the *Titanic*, September 11 2001, Area 51 and the creation of toothpaste.

---

*Not related to the Fibbers, a secret revolutionary organization from Wendover.

There is a growing trend to weave fanciful stories, which play shamelessly with Christian beliefs and ancient legends. There is no respect for history and they deny the truth, the authenticity of the Christian faith.

Father Raniero Cantalamessa
Pope Benedict XVI's personal priest
(Quoted *The Daily Mail* April 16 2006)

That's a bit rum coming from him! Has he not heard of the Council of Nicea?* (et al) Or the condemnation of Gnosticism – e.g. The Mandeans (a Gnostic sect from Iraq – Aramaic *mandaya* Gnostics, from *manda*, knowledge), with their alternative view of Jesus and the fevered rejection of the Nag Hammadi scrolls and so on. Notice the odd use of 'history' and 'deny the truth'. If religions can make things up, and that is all they have done, you certainly can. Thoroughly check your chosen historical milieu in terms of legalities, particularly in respect of those who hold the trademark for certain events.

Your local library should have a comprehensive list of historical situations now protected under the *Publishing Conspiracies in Literature Act* (1996). Try where you can to pick time periods that are little known, or have few facts focused on them. The earlier and more ancient the better. It is still unclear who it was that brought the Americas to the attention of Europe. Have your group responsible for such

---

*An ancient city in Asia Minor. There were two Councils of Nicea, the first being in 325 AD convened by Constantine and the second in 787 AD under Empress Irene. In short, the tenets of Christianity were cobbled together there.

an event or at least have them operating covertly in the background as, for example, patrons of an expedition. Be careful here not to tread on the toes of the Knights Templar who, it is now claimed, are the true discoverers of America – putting aside the Vikings, Christopher Columbus and more importantly the indigenous peoples of that land, who knew all about the place anyway. (Note: All this does is reveal a continuing Western bias in history.)

Patterns in a Landscape

Ruins and spurious points of interest on the landscape, if you are able, and this can often be seen as a real tour de force, can be linked up to form some meaningful pattern loaded with symbolism. We humans, particularly conspiracy theorists, love patterns: the more exaggerated and dynamic, the better. Pattern recognition is something that is hot-wired into the brain so exploit that part of neuroscience to your benefit. More importantly have the pattern (or don't hold back, patterns) represent something – usually, but not always, some symbol familiar to those who practise the occult. Pentagrams are the most obvious, but they are also now very much clichéd and a somewhat overdone image. Ignore them if you can. More often than not the pentagrams themselves are vague and have undoubtedly been forced to fit major landmarks so on the whole fail to fulfil that which was asked of them. Of course if you are going to develop a religious secret society you can employ these occult images as propaganda and agit-prop to instill wild and misplaced fears in people that something nefarious is abroad in the land – usually in the form of a Freemason.

Freemasons have born the brunt of such fevered negative press throughout their history. Some would have us believe that they all sport huge black moustaches, which they incessantly twiddle, carry round fizzing metal spheres with the word 'bomb' written on them and revel in congregating in numerous back rooms to plot the fall of just about anyone who crosses their path. Of course, when that happens to your secret society you will know that you have made it into the big league and you can look forward to years of ridiculous religious and media denigration.

In his controversial novel *Sunsphere*, with its now infamous shoot-out in a Masonic lodge scene, the author Mark Ardin utilises the golden ball atop the spire of the Church of St Lawrence near West Wycombe, constructed by our old chum Francis Dashwood to add spice to his best-selling story. Dashwood had modelled his sphere on the golden ball that can be seen gracing the Dogana Di Mari in Venice. It is well known that within the golden ball of St Lawrence there are a number of seats and Ardin makes great play of a similar set up in the one that caps that splendid Italian building. The Venetian one though is protected by traps of intricate cunning and contains a great secret that has remained hidden for centuries.

'Some distance below he could hear the tremulous sounds of idle chatter fluid in its melodious Italian cadence, describing the humdrumness, the ordinary, and the familiar. Businessmen negotiating last minute deals with merchants, the shouts of oarsmen, bosuns, or itinerant sailors looking to be hired for a ship's crew. Crass insults and friendly banter echoed along the ancient city walls against which the lapping of the water created an undulating hypnotically spasmodic rhythm with the taut creaking of rigging and the crack and flap of sail tugged by a night breeze rich in aromas of exotic spices from distant foreign lands that lay abroad.

'It was an obvious place to hide deep secrets but with an element of arrogance to it. A golden round sphere supported on two carved figures for all to see; perched high above and in plain view out of sight on the roof of the Venice Custom House with its statue of Fortune casting her mute blessings down upon the opulent but semi-drowned city.

'He reached into a weather worn pocket and pulled out a small key no longer than his small finger. At its head was an ornate sun-like symbol that had fine radiating lines spreading from its circumference. It was gold in colour but was obviously not forged in that element. It was certainly heavy for its size but he had seen and coveted enough of the precious substance in his time to realise that the key was fashioned in another metal. Not that it mattered. All he wanted was to find the lock built somewhere into the sphere.

'Pulling himself up he positioned his wiry frame beneath the ornamental sun and began running his ruddy hands around its surface hunting some obvious seam or opening in which to insert the key. Finding nothing obvious he paused to think. His mind flashed briefly to the tattered manuscript replete with clues, half-truths and hidden meanings, many of which he had failed to decipher. One page flashed into his mind's eye, a fine ink representation of the Sunsphere. He remembered that there was a small triangular mark above the equator and in the western half of the hemisphere. He shifted his attention to that part of the sphere and after a few moments found what he was looking for.

'He ran a fingertip along the gentle triangular depression in the surface. It was probably an inch and a half along each side and felt as if it might give beneath firm enough pressure. His hand balled into a fist for a moment with the tension. Then he unwound his fingers with rapid slowness. He closed his eyes and pressed with his regular left thumb.

'There was a deafening soft click then something sprung up and pierced the skin. He recoiled but he knew he was too late. The poison was fast acting. He took a step back, his mind already in a fog as dense as that which lay on the waters of the Grand Canal. He felt his throat close tightly and his muscles begin to tighten.

'His eyes rolled up and the light of a thousand distant suns, the high heavens above him full of stars that were suns, span as he tumbled from the roof of brown tiles of deep russet. For a brief second before the light of life was extinguished he stared wide-eyed into the infinite and saw a flash of lightning.

'The key slipped from his hand and tumbled; lamplight spilling and sparking across its surface as it spun in freefall. It bounced once on the street below before dropping unseen into the dark wet waters of the Grand Canal.'

What Ardin manages to do successfully is link, via Dashwood's architectural proclivities, two real locations into a

42

grand conspiratorial mystery. Where you can, you must follow Dashwood and Ardin's lead. Note: Everyone loves a mystery!

Plain truth will influence half a score of men at most in a nation, or an age, while mystery will lead millions by the nose.

Viscount Henry St John Bolingbroke

Mysteries, like religion, are the conjunction between dubious fact and lurid fallacy. But who gives a monkey's? It's profitable.

Mark Ardin, Interview in
Secret Society User, June 2003

See *The Holy Blood and the Holy Grail* by Lincoln, Baigent and Leigh, *Tomb of God* by Richard Andrews and Paul Schellenberger, and *Genisis* (sic): *The First Book of Revelations* by David Wood for examples of this approach. South west France, made popular by the above books, is a now exhausted location for great secrets (apparently) so think of somewhere new to base your geomantic fancies.

Buildings such as the great European cathedrals are built around sacred geometry. This idea has popped up again more recently in connection with Rosslyn Chapel, which is said to be based on a Templar cross (similar in design to the Maltese one). Numerous carvings within the chapel itself are claimed by some to be clues to a great secret. Chartres Cathedral is also said to be heaving with mystical codings and some have claimed that it's the resting place of the Ark of the Covenant (just how many resting places are there?).

Great Works of Art

If landscapes are not your thing then try paintings instead. Hiding secret messages in art is a great way to announce your arrival especially if you can concoct vast amounts of spurious 'sacred geometry' based around a famous image. Avoid where you can Da Vinci's *The Last Supper* and Poussin's *The Shepherds of Arcadia* as they have already been snapped up. Try instead George Stubbs' *Baboon and Albino Macaque Monkey* or Mark Rothko's *Black on Maroon*.

Caveat: When researching in libraries, be warned that many of these establishments now mix pseudo-science and false-history in with the genuine articles. This can be troublesome. Sifting fact from bogus eyewash can be a shrill experience and it certainly makes deciding what to use a difficult prospect. Pyramids as stargates and Stone Age astronauts sit side by side with the Russian Revolution (itself not immune from accusations of being started by meddling secret societies) and the Franco-Prussian War of 1870–71.

Ultimately, then, we get the past we deserve. In every generation, thinkers, writers, scholars, charlatans, and kooks (these are not necessarily mutually exclusive categories) attempt to cast the past in an image either they or the public desire or find comforting. We deserve better and can do better than weave a past from the whole cloth of fantasy and fiction.

Kenneth L. Feder
Frauds, Myths, and Mysteries:
Science and Pseudoscience in Archaeology, 1986

There is, frankly, a considerable amount of fake history around at the moment. A good rule of thumb is to look at the title. If the book has 'conspiracy', 'code', 'hidden', 'heresy', 'legacy', 'holy', 'treasure', 'deception', 'revelation', 'scroll(s)', 'secret', 'blood', 'sign' and 'key' on its cover, it is most likely a big bag of thoroughly nonsensical guff. Check the book blurb. Another give-away is the use of the word 'explosive' in the tag line: 'explosive new bestseller'. More importantly, this kind of 'literature' should be avoided because someone has plundered history for his or her own financial gain and to have your secret society associated with that is, at least initially, deeply frowned upon or worse, ridiculed. Besides, those authors got there first. History itself is replete with twaddle, propaganda, rewritten events, whether political or religious, and enough self-congratulatory nonsense as it is. Verisimilitude is a rare thing. Be circumspect.

The upside of all this is that some important questions are being asked of accepted, so called facts, particularly those relating to religion. This in itself is an important area to mine for source material. We only have to see the rattled wasps' nest that is Christianity after the publication of the Judas Scroll and the questions it has raised and the fevered rejection in theological circles that has followed on its revelatory heels.

One recent book that raced up the best-seller list, entitled *The Michaelangelo Syndrome* (with its now infamous gaudy type face), claimed that the eponymous artist had developed the rotary engine; was repeatedly abducted by aliens from Alpha Centauri; had sung in a flamenco a cappella band; and had written all of Da Vinci's best gags during his stand up period in Florence (despite the well known fact that both men could not stand the sight of each other). This casual flaunting of history is at best beyond daft and heading into the realms of the enormously silly. The author, who shall remain nameless, also claims Michaelangelo was a member of a secret society called *The Reluctant Crevices*, when in fact he was a third degree initiate of *The Alans*, a group who consisted entirely of gentlemen called Tommaso Salutati Sforza.

The Name Game

Some form of celebrity endorsement never goes amiss, but make sure of your facts before attaching a well-known name to your cause. Study carefully any known figure in history before you commit them to your 'back story'. Leonardo Da Vinci is the de rigueur character of choice at the moment. But was he, as some claim, involved in a secret society?

(Giovan Francesco Rustici) and Leonardo soon became close friends, prompting the latter's initiation into a mock fraternity created by Rustici called the Company of the Cauldron. Members met over copious quantities of wine and designed paintings and sculptures made entirely from food.

Michael White,
Leonardo The First Scientist, 2000

No Priory of Sion this! Da Vinci was not the kind of fellow who would be drawn into anything more conspiratorial

than the Company of the Cauldron. He was also, by definition, someone who was bordering on, in the modern
terminology, atheism at least in terms of a personal god. He
was not interested in magic or the occult. The 'holy' was not
really his bag, although he was steeped in the Christian
milieu at the time and painted religious imagery for money.
More importantly Da Vinci could never stick at anything for
too long so being a Grand Master and running a secret
society would have been a complete waste of his time and
there was too much to do. The great man also had a less
widely known personality trait – a splendid sense of
humour, which may explain a number of so-called
'mysteries' (if there are any of course). Was he simply having
a joke with us?

Being very slapdash and non-circumspect can lead you
into all kinds of academic hot water. The last thing you want
is some history swot informing you of your mistake about
the historical figure you have built your premise upon. Of
course no one can really deny, in the final analysis, whether
or not your character was involved in some secret society
but do your homework. Research everything you can about
the personages you wish to see associated with your group.
Then any criticism can be met with a swift and accurate
rejoinder aimed at demolishing any accusations of dimwittedness or slack reading on your behalf.

To Be or Not to Be Seen

Oxymoronic as it may seem some secret societies like to
make their presence known – especially those with an overt

political or religious agenda. The Holy Vehm (Germany), The Garduna (Spain) and The Decided Ones of Jupiter the Thunderer (Italy) were all secret societies who tended for the more *'here we are, look at our weapons'* approach. Whereas the likes of Freemasons, the Illuminati, the Ordines, the Assassins, the Hellfire Club and the Himalayan Masters all tended to keep themselves to themselves.

How you approach the world at large depends primarily on what kind of secret society you are trying to establish and the parameters of your political or religious agenda. Do you wish your presence known to the serried ranks of the great unwashed (for whatever purpose) or do you wish to keep your activities to the peace and quiet of the lodge, garden party or golf match?

Gabriel Blowne, the well-versed and well-walked traveller spent many years trying to find the truths behind stories of the lesser-known secret societies that were rumoured to exist throughout England. It seems one group had opted for the latter course of action by keeping their activities extremely secret. All this subsequently did was fuel the notion that they were in fact so quiet that they did not really exist at all, except in the fevered imaginings of the local peasants.

In his book *The Secret Men* (1758), a sequel to the barn-storming *The Man Who Blew Too Much*, Gabriel Blowne described hearing of *'certaine men named the Beastes'*, during the latter half of his tour of England in 1756. He had set out to find more about this brotherhood, a singular cadre called the *Withy Beasts*, of which little is known even today, but failed in his duty to do so. In this extract Blowne spends a short time enquiring of the whereabouts of this under-ground movement in a less than palatial inn.

'I took myself of my own personal avail to return onto the hills of the county where in recent years I had stumbled innumerable times in a discordant manner out over the threshold of the Derbyshire Gibbon, a fine Inn somewhere within in a ten mile radius of Frampton Camcorder, to explore the various byways of those fine embonpointed upwellings of moundalur limestonic strata. This village had taken upon itself to move on various occasions from said county of Somersetshire and I last heard that it had settled lately in a fine resplendent visage outside the hamlet of Two Horns near Farleyford Wynd. So on this occasion I facilitated myself of an easy egress from the promptostical salutations of the heavily wainscoted lavatories of the Deliberate Monster, my new Inn of choice on that particular day from which to begin my rustic peregrinations in quest of certaine men named the Beastes.

'Being of stout amplitude and of vigorous verisimilitudinal countenance and indeed having polished my whethers, I reasoned that in light of my recent wholesome cessation of suspended and rudimentary opines that I disencumber myself with previously held fragulations of a colestomical nature. In that such sensibilities held, within the confines of a needless rousing, enable one to forego certain frumptotic stalations of the mind and regale the thoughts with tremulous mental aberrational singularities.

'In conversational ejaculation with certain dyspeptic and frightfully ruddy gentlemen of whom one may say that in their stature they were seldom of an upright nature due in part to the consummation of lurid quantities of heavily brewed drinkages and also in part due to their inability to remove themselves, unless to engage in the rough sport of face-aching, from the damp boudoirs of their lodges, I was sorely regaled with intrigues and machinational impromptitudes as to warrant my near evacuation. Such men, I warranted, were of disproportionately ignoble infamy and were known to frighten certain vaporous ladies of the parish of Wells, disporting and derobing themselves in a frockular nature beyond that which was deemed wholesome and necessarily emblematic of the county.

'Therein, within the gambrelled nook of a sturdy port of call named The Mistimed Thrutch in which I sought some solace, a certain squalidinous gentlemen (of whom, in passing I had failed to repel with such vivid fistular manipulations), awash I might say in clouds of tobacconistic cumulus, disembogued himself of certain populastic inoctitudes. I took him to be nothing more than a mountebank and rustic pettifogger, perhaps a Shipham lightweight such were his glossetings. His accidental disportments had left him with crude manifestations of his previous wayward indignities but his frasmotic emollients were nevertheless forthcoming and I purchased for him, in serried ranks, a great multitude of aleous beverages of which was comprised, in the most part, of a salacious inoculent called Colonic BeDevilment.

'Soon my conversational rectitudes were not dissimilar to that of a man of lesser standing, due in part to the festitudes of the drink, and I demanded of him news of the cadre in question upon which our longitudinal meanderings had happened upon and of which activities had brought me. With immodest peripatetic disectitudes he uttered a deleterious barrage of dispompic gloatings but vowed thereon to disport me to the threshold of lodgings of the Withy Beastes.'

Blowne never made it. He was set upon by a gang of swarthy cutthroats who "...*kicked me full hard about the bag.*" Blowne never returned to that part of the country and was to write in his diary of that period that he feared that the attack was nothing more than a tactic to scare him off from his quest. He may very well have been right.

Secular or Ecumenical?

> *The quickest way to make money it is said is*
> *to create a religion. The quickest way to create*
> *a stink is to set up a secret society.*

Lord Horace Smeng
Why I became a Prancer (1964)
Collected correspondences from the trial

Further consideration must be made towards the spiritual nature, if any, of your secret society. This will have direct bearing on the type, procedures, initiations, regalia, methodology, credo and behaviour of your cabal. It is safe to say that all the conflict in the world today is about the two Rs – religion and resources – the former often used to acquire the latter, e.g. the recent Gulf Wars – god and oil – being the most obvious modern example. Keep this in mind while creating your secret society, if you choose the religious path, as it will play an important part in deciding your agenda.

The most deliberate and venomous antagonism will come, more often than not, from established religions who will see your activities as nothing short of Devil-worship and your cadre as the bulwark of the anti-christ: Satan. Or more importantly that you worship a 'god' that is not their one, such as the Freemasons' *Jahbulon*, a name created from Jahweh, Bul or Baal and On or Osiris. Martin Short in his book *Inside the Brotherhood* states that they are '...*the names of three pre-Christian deities, some with Satanistic overtones.*' A somewhat silly notion as in a pre-Christian Hebrew world 'Satan' just meant an adversary, as it is in the Islamic faith. This is what 'Jesus' meant when he said to Peter, '*Get behind me, Satan!*' (Matt 16: 23). One of the gods is not even from the Hebrew tradition, where no Satan exists. This is just another way to accuse the Freemasons of cavorting with 'dark forces' or of being nothing more than Devil worshippers. Anyway, if you want to worship another god that is indeed your business. People worship different deities right across the world – are they all wrong? Can they all be right?

Despite the frenetic carping of certain quarters of the first and fourth estates we are not living in a secular age nor is science in its twilight period as some loons have it ([don't] see John Horgan's silly book *The End of Science*) – quite the contrary. Religion, the pseudo-sciences and anti-science all rule supreme. How many people look up their 'stars' in the paper every day? How many actually look up at the real stars above their heads? A far more exiting and worthwhile activity. The narrow-minded and illiberal attempts to quash free-thinking with the use of childish homilies, quaint fairy tales, myths, legends and heavy handed threats while ignoring the facts, increase year after year. Remember religion has done enough to damage its reputation over the millennia but still needs its scapegoats. You will be one of those! It is worth noting that all religions started as cults and secret cabals but you try telling them that and you will get nothing but swift and repeated kicks up the backside, such as those seen in Charlie Chaplin movies.

> *Organised religion is a sham and a crutch for the*
> *weak-minded people who need strength in numbers.*
> *It tells people to go out and stick their noses in*
> *other people's business…*

Jesse Ventura
Governor of Minnesota

For a subject that is orientated to the left of the political spectrum – love, harmony; peace; respect your neighbour's ox, wife, dog; do not fight, kill, murder; help your fellow man, woman, child – religion is a hot bed of right wingers and extremists who want to shoot or hang everybody. One only has to witness the activities of certain beige Christian folk as they try to noisily park their cars outside their church, to the accompaniment of much swearing and door slamming, to see that the love their fellow man is indeed a sham. Certainly all religions do have their softer side but it is always puzzling to see right wingers adhering to something that is essentially a left wing ideology. Why, for example, does the Catholic Church have an essentially right wing newspaper and a more liberal one? i.e. *The Herald* and the *Tribune*. Mind you, there's a Christian newspaper called *The Universe*, which makes no sense whatsoever – or is, at the very least, spectacularly presumptive. Maybe it's an Islamic universe or a Buddhist one. Or perhaps, and this is more likely, it's a good old scientific one.

> *Jesus is the only leftie*
> *Worshipped by the right…*
> *Jesus is the only leftie…*
> *Prayed to by the right…*

Claybert Frankenthrash III
Country and Western Singer

All of this must be taken into consideration when deciding the cut and thrust of your credo. Will you take the Hellfire Club route and put the wind up the Church or will you follow the path taken by the Holy Vehm, metering out fiery retribution to anyone who pauses to question the Bible. Remember many humans will kill to defend the non-existent. Will you?

If you take the atheist approach, then look out! This will really put the proverbial cat amongst the pious pigeons. Atheists, like scientists, are blamed for all the supposed increase in immorality, selfishness, social failures and crime. Yes, of course, it is silly but you must be on the ball as to what the opposition believes. The Church usually refers to an 'atheist conspiracy', but have yet to put this down in novel form. Of course, you won't buy it because it has the word 'conspiracy' in the title. If you decide to add 'liberal' to your atheist or scientific stance, then wow!, you really are going to have some fun.

*His faith in the supernatural was starting
to get but verily on my Bristols!*

Frederick Fock, 1757
The Stations of the Charing Cross

It is often great fun to watch the reactions of evangelists, often at your door, as they are told that they are talking to an atheist who is content with life. There is always a look of total bemusement on their puzzled faces. This is because they are told that anyone who does not believe in a deity must be a miserably wretched soul in dire need of rescuing. Burst the fantasy balloons of those silly believers! You can be happy and not worship a mythical entity.

*[Supernatural beliefs] fail to do justice to
the sublime grandeur of the real world...*

Richard Dawkins

These believers are certainly a funny lot. Cop this loon! Judge Braswell Dean of Georgia Court of Appeals stated in 1981: '*This monkey mythology of Darwin is the cause of permissiveness, promiscuity, pills, prophylactics, perversions, pregnancies, abortions, pornography, pollution, poisoning, and proliferation of crimes of all types.*' Most of these have been around since the dawn of time, of course, and religion has failed to stop any of them. Who though would want to stop pregnancies? (Or indeed most of that list.) None of us would be here!

You can if you wish focus your praise on the following people: Carl Sagan, James Randi, Michael Shermer, Charles Darwin, Daniel Dennett, Isaac Asimov, John Lennon, Sir Arthur C. Clarke, Allen Ginsberg, Albert Einstein, Julian Huxley, Peter Ustinov, Gore Vidal, Kurt Vonnegut Jr., William Carlos Williams, Arthur Miller.

Alternatively, you are a modern day Canute who wants to turn the unstoppable secular tide, feeling that the world is going to Hell in a handcart and that the reasons for this are the troublesome and meddling scientists (and atheists) who are criticising and tearing down all your hallowed beliefs with their facts, measurements and logic. Or more importantly, and heaven forbid, other forms of worship are getting in the way! Okay, what are you going to do about it? Well most religions are happy to carry on launching broadsides of fire and brimstone every once in a while but is that enough? Your answer will, of course, be 'No'. You may feel that most religious bodies are not up to the job of defending your particular brand of faith. Despite the best efforts of evangelists, whether in the press or on very late night unwatchable chitchat programmes, the message is being lost. Time then, for some affirmative action. You have two approaches to the problem and it is entirely up to you which direction you decide to go.

A charitable organisation: Offering assistance, inclusiveness, brother or sisterhood, benevolence, spreading of the word of the deity, crochet evenings, tea, jam making, hug-ins.

Militant: Pick up that bloody sword and run the atheist bastards through!

In recent years there has been a dramatic up turn in the second option in all religious outlets. As science has made great headways into understanding the way the universe works all 'faiths' find themselves having to resort to violence and aggressive measures, sometimes even the use of sneery journalists. If that's for you, go for it. You could even try and recruit these bombastic scribes to your ranks so that you have an outlet for your propaganda. The right wing press is best for this, as their level of scientific understanding is minimal at best although the left is often equally guilty of such.

Avoid using creationism or the equally daft 'intelligent design' (which is just creationism spun through a PR machine) in the tenets of your secret society. It is a devalued and bogus belief system that has been rightly ridiculed. Like the idea of the flat Earth, the jungles of Venus and the Austin Allegro, it should be consigned to history. There is no point demeaning yourself with such fallacies. It will be tough enough trying to get yourself established, so do not sabotage this delicate time with the use of silly ideas. Even the Church accepts Evolution now, so you would be unwise not to do the same. (On October 27 1996, Pope John Paul in an address to the Pontifical Academy of Sciences in Rome said as much.) Farmers in the Bible belt of the United States will happily deny evolution but will curse to high heaven and wonder why the insects they persistently try to eliminate are resistant to their pesticides year after year. Do not aspire to that same level of dimwittedness. Deniers of evolution find the errors in science then denounce all science as being wrong – watch your step.

For those of you wishing to set up a religious order here's a checklist of enemies:

Atheists
Scientists
Gnostics
Worshippers of different deities
Liberals
Lefties
Homosexuals
Occultists
Satanists
Heavy Metal rock musicians (Death Metal, a hot
  favourite)
Communists
Buddhists
Jews
Swarthy foreigners
Teachers
Freemasons
Hollywood
Richard Dawkins
Marilyn Manson
Or any combination of the above.

Fear not. Some scientists believe in a deity. You will often find those attached to universities funded from the coffers of evangelist organisations or cults. Be sure to look them up and get them on board with your creed. Avoid where you can the more prestigious colleges and pick only those from the American Mid-West and Deep South.

You can if you wish focus your ire and brimstone on the following people: Carl Sagan, James Randi, Michael Shermer, Charles Darwin, Daniel Dennett, Isaac Asimov,

John Lennon, Sir Arthur C. Clarke, Allen Ginsberg, Albert Einstein, Julian Huxley, Peter Ustinov, Gore Vidal, Kurt Vonnegut Jr., William Carlos Williams, Arthur Miller.

It should be noted that the Church of England has had a strong Masonic connection. Even the Roman Catholic Church (although despising them) had Freemasons in the Vatican (see David Yallop's *In God's Name*) so religion does not always equate with an anti-secret society stance. (Keep in mind though that Yallop made the odd statement that phone tapping is a particularly Masonic habit. How does he know? Has he been listening?)

Caveat: It is worth noting that you must remember to avoid paranoia as this can lead to no end of problematic trouble. Once that sets in you will find that you will have the urge to purchase a vast array of weaponry while sensing, perhaps, the call of the wild. You will also feel the need to add 'militia' to the name of your cabal, followed, eventually, by an almost irresistible desire to blame someone, often the prevailing government, of being in league with your enemy of choice, in most cases the Jews. Hot on the heels of this will be the prestigious and excessive use of explosives.

The Occult

The third way for a secret society to follow is that of the occult. One of the most famous examples of this was the Golden Dawn, a magic based cabal who kicked about during the early part of the 20th century chanting and evoking to no particular outcome other than to startle ladies of a mature age and outrage vicars into rigorous bouts of heated and red-faced apoplexy.

The beauty of an occult based secret society is that your imagination has free rein to do exactly what it wants. You can come up with and develop a credo and its rituals without influence from anywhere except your subconscious. Aleister Crowley, who made the Golden Dawn famous, was adept at using his libido as a source of his mystical workings and he could often be seen waving his wand around the front gardens of the ladies of the county, usually if they had a few quid stashed away somewhere.

There are plenty of books out there from which to source rituals and magic (not the producing balls in the hand kind). It is not unknown for some rituals to be euphemistically 'borrowed' and adapted from Christianity or the ever-popular and now frankly exhausted writings of Freemasonry.

Occult secret societies fall into two categories:

1. The working of rituals for selfish ends e.g. a nefarious will to power, sexual conquest, copping a feel.
2. The working of rituals for beneficial ends e.g. world peace, understanding, love, cheap beer.

Crowley himself ended his days in a tatty boarding house in Hastings, so use of the occult has its downside. Unless you want to spend your twilight years rotting in a seaside town you may wish to avoid using certain incantations – if you choose to utilise the Crowley-esque series of rituals that is. Rule of thumb: make up your own spells.

The Heady World of Finance

You may, of course, decide that money is your raison d'être. If racketeering, numbers, gambling, loan sharking, money laundering, pandering and fraud are your thing then the more business-orientated secret society is for you.

By its very nature money related cadres are, on the whole, not that secret, as they have to operate within the community at large from which they can make profit. Threatening late payers also means that people will know exactly who you are. Discretion is not something readily thought of as a necessary asset. Should the legal profession catch up with you then be prepared for a lot of media attention, although learning the gentle arts of bribery and blackmail will assist in removing any unnecessary attention. Note: Not all bribery and blackmail actions need a monetary base. This is when learning the skill of photography comes in handy.

In this realm there are no secrets per se but there is always a hierarchy; a ranking system in which new comers, after initiation, make their way up the levels to become criminal bosses. There is also a swearing of allegiance and, unlike other secret societies, death threats tend to be carried out, so be prepared for such eventualities. Powerful membership – initiating those in high places – is an absolute must for the fiscal based cabal. The legal profession is also a good source for recruitment – for obvious reasons.

This form of secret society is perhaps the most difficult to develop and sustain. Competition is tough. The financial world is a real minefield. A number of bad eggs from other secret societies have dipped their toes in this realm and have come severely unstuck. Be careful. The best examples of this particular brand of secret society are the Mafia, Tongs, Yakuza and the Triads. The major banks also claim a major stake hold in this particular sphere as well.

Fear

> *Quem metuunt, oderunt.*
> (They hate whom they fear.)

Ennius, 239–169 BC

Fear, as the title of the 1972 film has it, is the Key. Fear is a useful tool employed by politicians, priests and the commercial world to get us to do things we would not normally do. Fear is a primitive survival instinct, but one that can be exploited to a devastating effect.

In terms of secret societies fear can be employed two ways.

1. By those seeking to demean the secret society in the eyes of the public.
2. By the secret society wishing to gain power.

Critics of your cabal will use fear to instill in the population at large the idea that you are a threat to the established political or religious status quo. In many respects it does not matter whether you are or not, depending on your agenda of course, out to do harm to either the Church or State. Even the most benign of organisations have been given an air of menace that can subsequently be exploited by men of power, God or conspiracy theory. The Odd Fellows, RAOB and the Ordines have all suffered such dubious honour. Article 22 of Hamas' covenant has the Rotarians, Freemasons and the Lions behind the French Revolution, Communism and the invasion of Iraq.

On the other hand fear is a damn fine and useful tool that can be employed to get people off your back. Off hand remarks that contain veiled threats are often enough to send a bitter critic scuttling for the shadows. It also certainly helps in fuelling the notion that your order has power where none actually (as yet) exists. By developing fear you can build up genuine kudos for your ensemble. It will also attract further criticism from those out to scupper your plans, which in the long run can only be of benefit – it becomes a well-regulated machine. Fear begets criticism, which begets kudos and then power that generates more fear. Take a hefty leaf out of the book of politics and religion and exploit this most basic of human emotions.

The Profane

All non-members of your organisation. This word is derived from the Latin words *pro*, meaning 'before' and *fanum*, meaning the 'temple'. The profane are therefore 'those outside the temple' who are ignorant of what goes on inside. Those who are not 'initiated'.

It is from them that much of your criticism will come but be aware that they are also a useful tool for propagating the myths, urban legends and conspiracy theories that will adhere to your organisation.

Charitable Behaviour

You may of course choose to help your fellow man, including the profane, in acts of charity. This is in the bailiwick of only a handful of societies – the Odd Fellows being the most famous. Charitable and education societies were prominent in 19th century America.

Resurrection Time!

So, that's the basic groundwork out of the way. Now you are ready to cross that threshold – or as the lingua franca of the world you are entering has it; you are about to be '*raised*', '*initiated*' or '*resurrected*' into a new life.

> *Those who say they will die first and then rise are in error*
> *They must receive the resurrection while they live…*

> *The Gospel of Philip*

II

In Which the Requirements
are Discussed.

I must create a system,
or be enslaved by another Man's…

William Blake, *Jerusalem*

The Inner Workings
and Establishing the Craft

Now we move into what goes on behind closed doors. You have decided on the direction, type, agenda and make up of your secret society. Now you need to make decisions concerning the inner workings of your cabal. As trivial as this sounds you must pay particular attention to this side of your affairs.

The Grand Master

In the primary stages of your secret society it is wise to adopt the mantle of Grand Master yourself. This simple action leaves no doubt in the eager minds of newcomers that it is to you that they are beholden – should you choose to adopt that stance. Some Grand Masters choose to facilitate a more avuncular approach towards those in their charge, while others favour the more despotic milieu. It is recommended that you favour the former but are ready to adopt the latter should dissension in the ranks occur. You may like to consider having that position indefinitely, perhaps until you have shuffled off this mortal coil. A more equitable situation would be to hand over the reins after a set period of time, but there is nothing to say that you cannot become a 'leader of men' for as long as you please. It is, after all is said and done, your organisation. This attitude tends to be prevalent in the cult circuit and on the whole is frowned upon in the more serious fraternal brotherhoods that exist throughout the world.

After several years of service you may opt to step down and become a past master thus allowing a favoured second, the Grand Master in waiting, to take on the role. How they achieve this position is entirely up to you. It is often accepted practice that the Grand Master can only be considered for the position once he has served in all the offices of the lodge. This is certainly an idea that has its merits. If a Grand Master wants to oversee a lodge he must have full understanding of how it works. Now this may take many years – in that each position taken in turn may occupy a man for as many as five, ten, fifteen, even twenty years. But at least when his time comes he will have honoured the lodge by his commitment and dedication and is therefore extremely worthy of the moniker and position of Grand Master.

Suitable candidates must be considered wisely. It is sometimes the case that a Grand Master may attain his desired goal of running a lodge but will then set about enforcing his will on others to the detriment of the lodge. This can be disconcerting to all but the most thick-skinned. (See section on Bad Eggs.) Should this ever happen there must be policies and contingencies in place to remove him from the chair.

A Grand Master must not take up the position until he has served all the other important roles within the lodge. By doing this he will understand the entire workings of the lodge and the secret society at large. Even so, by undertaking to perform all those duties this will not guarantee the big chair. Other high-ranking members of the lodge will be asked to vote on a suitable candidate when the position of Grand Master becomes available. They will, of course, rate him on his behaviour up until that point. If he has failed in his duties he will not receive the top position. Voting should be done in secret by whatever means or methods you deem worthy.

Normally the proposed candidate would have spent the previous year (or whatever time frame you decide) holding the rank of 'Vice Grand Master' (not meant to sound naughty!) or 'Grand Master in Waiting' or 'Vice Chair' – the name is entirely of your choosing. After this set period the present Grand Master will call to order and notify that the time of his presidency is nearing completion and that the time is nigh to elect a new Grand Master.

> *Brother, I call upon your good nature and to stand beside me as we deem our solid companion who is of stout heart and of good measure the position of Grand Cuckoo. Using your skill and judgement elect the said man to his calling or do not. Quack!*

> Grand Cuckoo's Proclamation
> The Loyal Order of the Men of Gotham

In the Freemasons the man responsible for the lodge is the Worshipful Master and the Grand Master is the fellow who oversees all the lodges in a region or country. You may wish to adopt this moniker instead.

Duties

The Grand Master, as well as running the lodge, will have such outside duties as liaising with other lodges – should you be lucky to have your secret society blossom into a national institution. He will be, in all respects, the public face of your organisation and if not public, then at least a figure head to maintain order, discipline and the smooth running of the craft. He will, of course, be the person responsible for ceremonies, including the initiation of acolytes as well as the raising to higher ranks of extant members.

The Grand Master will not be responsible for your secret society's policies. These must already be laid down in your charter (see below). The Grand Master will not dictate changes to this document or any tenets contained therein. He may suggest likely additions or amendments, but nothing more. Any long term and serious alterations to your credo must be hotly debated and worked through. Consultation with your fellow members is a must. This is your secret society, but you now have people loyal to your cause and they must be respected. (Unless you go the despot route.)

Charter and Constitutions

The rules, regulations, ceremonies and other sundries, drawn up into one document. You may wish to be entirely responsible for this or you may, if your fraternal organisation is more egalitarian, ask your inner circle for suggestions.

It is recommended that the charter is written up and bound in an impressive book made from very thick expensive paper or vellum with a heavy leather cover – a title is optional. This gives it an authentic feel with added gravitas. It should be kept in a large chest preferably near the hub of your ceremonies. If you get stuck most banks will look after them for you. Should your secret society spread then keep the charter at the first lodge that is set up: i.e. '*Lodge 1*', the '*Casa Princeps*'.

Grand Masters of other lodges who wish to discuss adapting the charter should address all correspondences to Lodge number one – i.e. you. On no account must they make changes without your authority, unless they decide to splinter off to start their own secret society. Grand Masters who want to set up a new lodge in your order must put their wishes in (coded) writing to you. Their lodge designation will be sequentially numbered from the previous one set up. They may also give their lodge a name. There are no problems with that, as such, but any name must be reasonable. You may require them to run the epithet by you for confirmation of suitability.

In the 1720s various spasms rocked the Freemasons, as there were claims of '*irregular assemblies*' or clandestine lodges in defiance of the set Regulations. This was due in part to certain Masons who felt dissatisfied by the absolute authority of the Grand Lodge. Anthony Sayer, the first Grand Master of all English Masons, was hauled before his superiors and given a sound ticking off as a result.

Make sure this does not happen to you. Be considerate and understanding to the wishes of your membership or you may have a rebellion to deal with. On the other hand do not be swayed by every whim that comes your way, whether it is your own or that of a fellow lodge member.

The Constitution of the Freemasons was written up in 1723 by one James Anderson and comprised of Charges and General Regulations and a detailed history of the 'art of Freemasonry' and its symbolism. Consult it if you are able.

Offices of the Lodge

How many of these are needed? Well, initially not many but as your society grows in stature and numbers you will find that the official positions will increase. Do not worry at the early stage if you think you have too few. At the beginning you will not have enough members to fill a large number of roles anyway. The time duration for each position held is at your discretion.

You will of course have a Grand Master but you may wish to consider the following list of offices for inclusion. What you call each office is again down to personal choice.

Grand Master. May run your lodge or oversee many lodges.

Worshipful Master. In charge of the ceremonies and lodge matters.

Past Master. The last Grand Master who is there in an advisory capacity.

Grand Master/Worshipful Master in Waiting. The next person for the big chair.

Protector of the Gate★. There to admit or refuse members, visitors, gate crashers, prying media or religious representatives of a frenetic nature. Usually has a drawn sword.

Chief Steward. Runs the lodge during dinner evenings, social events etc.

Chief Steward in Waiting.

Treasurer. Looks after those all important funds you will need for whatever fiscal requirements are so deemed.

Ushers. Move visitors, initiates etc around.

Grubber+. Someone who empties the bins.

Pumper^. Someone who pumps.

The Freemasons also have the titles:

Inner Guard. Lets Masons in to the lodge.

Junior Deacon. Carries messages.

Senior Deacon. Carries more important messages.

★ The Freemasons call this the Tyler.
+ A *Petty Revellers* term.
^ From *The Aeolian Brotherhood*. The Pumper gets the wind ready.

Junior Warden. Calls everyone from 'work' to refreshment and vice versa.

Senior Warden. Closes the lodge.

Charity Steward. Looks after the donations.

Almoner. In charge of collecting and spending benevolent funds.

Director of Ceremonies. In charge of rituals.

Chaplain. Conducts the prayers.

All respect must be given to each office and each representative of that position must be treated accordingly and with due deference. Even the humblest rank must be afforded some degree of civility. One day the Grubber may become the Grand Master.

Regalia

No self-respecting secret society can do without something to dress up in. Although it is not de rigueur it often benefits the psychological mindset of the adherents and allows them to feel that bit more special. As with any club, organisation or society the feeling of continual self-improvement helps the secret society as a whole. Bonds of kinship are strengthened by the use of badges, pins, tags, sashes, coins, aprons and so on. The use of regalia also allows the initiate to feel part of something special (perhaps the most important aspect) and inspires in them the desire to progress through the ranks, learning more as they do so. As in military circles ambition for promotion is a keen motivator and, although not for the many, at least those desirous of improved status are willing to aspire to a new stripe or rank pip.

In the majority of people there is an urge to collect, gather and to horde, particularly in the male of the species. Whether it is miniature trains, stamps, Boy Scout badges, tea cards, bottle tops, toy cars or tin robots, the willingness to accumulate is neither diminished nor abated in adulthood. Your secret society should be able to offer and satiate that basic human trait by offering a varied selection of achievement or status paraphernalia. The nature and form of these items is once more entirely up to you, but consider the notion that it is both helpful for the continuation and the eternal loyalty of your cadre if there are a considerable number of these gewgaws.

There should be a badge, and the term is used in the broadest sense, for acolytes, initiates, and other ranks all the way up to the Grand Master (and beyond for those special secret societies). The suggestion is made that these items are less prestigious and simple for new recruits but that the style and execution of the higher status icons are of a more elaborate nature. For example, you may choose to have as your basic recognition symbol a metal circle, perhaps representing 'eternity', or the 'wheel of life'. At the basic acolyte level this will indeed be the simple circle but once the bearer has been raised into the next level the symbol will change through the addition of say a single wing, or a sun icon, or the use of the number '1'. This continues throughout the lifetime of the member with each new badge displaying the additional motif or icon concordant with the rank that the member has attained. The psychological impact this has cannot be understated. A rising sense of self worth and importance will increase as each new badge is earned.

Regalia may contain any of the following:

Pins
Badges
Gems
Coins
Epaulettes
Gauntlets
Chains of office
Aprons
Sashes
Hats
Blindfolds or 'Hoodwinks'
Lanyards
Handkerchiefs
Underwear
Broaches
Shoes
Knitwear
Conkers
Rings
Cufflinks
Drinking vessels
Combs

Watches
Hot water bottle covers
Scarves
Duvet covers
Fully posable action figures

All should increase in adornments as each level is attained.
In terms of how to dress within the lodge see Attire below.

Secrets

We dance round in a ring and suppose
But the Secret sits in the middle and Knows...

Robert Frost, *The Secret Sits*

The great Robert Frost there, but is he right? No secret
society worth its salt can do without its secrets. Now, are
they 'secret societies' or 'societies with secrets'? Well, they are
both and of course neither, depending on one's point of
view. To get to the underlying problem the notion of exactly
what their secrets could be must be analysed.

First thing's first.

By definition a secret society must be secret but the very
idea, in many respects, is something of an oxymoron. The
visibility of these societies is not obscured. One can walk
down the high street of many British towns and clearly see a
signpost pointing the way to the nearest Masonic lodge. The
magnificent building of The Grand Lodge in London is not
exactly hard to miss and one is unlikely to find oneself trip-
ping over it accidentally on a casual stroll along Great Queen
Street. This is not, in itself, a problem, but perhaps the
moniker of 'secret' must be dropped due to its constant and
continuing inaccuracy. Most, if not all 'secret' societies now
have websites, some of which are extremely well presented,

79

allowing an unprecedented access to at least the 'outer portal' of their institutions. Of course, one must resist the temptation to use the term 'fluffy' to describe the modern secret society, but at least they are making efforts to rid themselves of the conspiratorial mystique that has shrouded them for so long. (Of course, it should not be forgotten that this very same mystique has been nurtured by the very same people now apparently attempting to reverse the process.)

In reality a secret society should really be seen as a society with secrets. Numerous books, documentary films and so-called exposes in one form or another, mostly very silly it must be said, keep the general public aware of these brotherhoods. Hardly a month goes by without someone decrying Freemasonry, the Illuminati, the Ordines, Skull and Bones, Bohemian Grove and the Buffaloes as nothing more than a group of revolutionary Johnnies trying to bring down society or put the wind up the Church. The secrets they keep may bring about the downfall of humanity. Frankly, that is nonsense.

Your detractors will probably invent sinister secrets to tarnish your reputation. To keep your secrets safe you must maintain a noble and diplomatic silence. Unfortunately this very same silence will bring you to the attentions of the fevered speculators. The Knights Templar fell into this trap before they were extinguished. They were accused of all kinds of heinous and heretical activities but did nothing to dispel these accusations – to their detriment. Be on your guard but defend wisely!

So, what secrets to use?

Well the beauty of this is that the secret can be anything form the inane, bizarre to the downright revolutionary. It all depends on what kind of secret society you have opted to construct. Basically it is up to the individual to construct a valid set of 'secrets' that can inspire suitable reverence in those who have recently passed the first level of initiation. The secrets growing more impressive as each level is passed.

Secrets usually take the form of recognition grips, signs and special words that allow one member of the secret society to recognise the other. They can of course be large scale, from a five year plan to subvert a legal process, to instigating the downfall of a country's power base, plundering another nation's resources, or simply to make as much money as possible through insider dealing. Even the noble aim of the enlightenment of humanity should be considered. Of course, you do not have to be a member of a secret society to do any of the above. But it is beneficial to set goals.

Some of the most controversial secrets you can possess relate directly to religion – usually some source for its true origin or some lost gospel or manuscript. You can make great claims to be the true keepers of these secrets, but be sure to make them earth shattering or explosive. Using those kind of pejorative terms will have your opponents fuming with rage.

A number of sects, such as those connected to Gnosticism (from Gnosis, to know), had heretical beliefs about the nature of Christianity, the most famous being the Cathars. The 'orthodox' Church tried to extinguish these ideas because naturally enough they contradicted the carefully controlled, so-called facts that had become mainstream. Several documents have come to light in recent decades, like the alternative Gospels such as those written by Philip, Thomas and now Judas, which have all run counter, on the whole, to what the Church has taught. It would certainly be

fun to consider a lost Gospel relating to some other character from the New Testament to really ferment Church
antagonism towards your society.

Once more that pesky thing called science gets in the way.
Genuine secrets are those related to the workings of the
universe and careful research and study are slowly revealing
these. In truth, to call them secrets suggests they are being
kept that way by an outside force, but that is a nonsensical
concept. Science is taking us from ignorance to understanding but that should not stop you coming up with some
cracking ideas about our place in the grand scheme of things.

Caveat: Don't be too hasty to give away all your secrets
in one go. Save the really good ones for later, perhaps after
the final initiation ceremony when your acolyte had
ascended through the ranks and has reached the highest
level within the organisation. Even then it may be wise to
have a few more tucked away. Having secrets that are really
hush-hush keep even those at the top eager for more.
Freemasonry for example has three main levels after
'apprentice' and the Mason is 'raised' up the ranks to a Third
Degree. Most Freemasons only ever reach that stage and are
often unaware that there are another 30 degrees above
them. Or at least they used to be unaware, until the advent
of widespread publishing, the Internet and of course the
numerous books on the subject.

Three may keep a secret, if two of them are dead.

Benjamin Franklin

The nature of the secrets tend to fall into either:

Esoteric

The brotherhood has knowledge of certain aspects of the metaphysical or magical processes that can be employed for benefit of either the self or the organisation as a whole. A prime example of this would be the secrets of Alchemy; the ancient art of turning base metals into gold. Now we are well aware that turning lead into gold is well beyond the reach of a fledgling secret society and you are unlikely to have the means, money or in fact the place to carry out such methods. Use of alchemical terms could in fact be employed (at least in the early stages), as they frequently are, for the purposes of metaphor. The initiate, through self-improvement, turns him or herself from a crude base form mortal to an enlightened being by the very act of being a member of your secret society. This set of secrets tends to flame the ire of the established Church (historically Catholicism), who will accuse you of Devil worship and numerous heathen activities. Francis Dashwood was constantly the butt of incessant finger waving from apoplectic men of the cloth. But he cracked on apace with his thing. Do not be deterred!

Political

The brotherhood will put itself into certain positions within the community at all levels of the country's power base to ensure that certain ideologies and philosophies are carried out or encouraged. The secrets should be related to who those people are, and the positions of power they occupy; and the ideologies and long term plans and the resultant benefits. It is this second category of secrets that dominates the focus of conspiracy theorists who will, without failure, assume that your secret society is out to dominate and run the world (a now very dull and overused concept). These same people accuse the members of the Bohemian Grove and the Bilderberg organisation as having just that policy in mind. Why should yours be any different? Some very famous and successful men are members of these esteemed organisations.

A subset of the political form of 'secret' are those that encompass 'revolution'. Usually those on the Christian capitalist right* will accuse the Freemasons (always their particular cross to bear) of being behind all the major revolutions that have upset the world. Included in this list are the Illuminati who have also been accused of the same thing. Now there is nothing against the idea that certain revolutionaries were Freemasons especially in France, but to suggest that every unrest due to grim working, social and financial conditions was the work of a secret society is indeed somehow patronising of those keen to stand up for their basic human rights. One possible exception is the United States, whose revolution was born out of numerous and perfectly understandable reasons, not least heavy taxes – and who wants those? Many of those who signed the Declaration of Independence were indeed Freemasons. You should wherever possible avoid engaging in this kind of dramatic display though, especially in the fledgling years. Revolutions are tricky things to handle and often use belli-

*It is interesting to note that Jesus, if he existed, did behave the way it is said he did in the Bible then he, too, would have been labelled a 'leftie' revolutionary. More so if he engaged in that activity in the modern world. It is interesting to note that an iconic left wing figure has become a symbol of the right.

cose activities to garner a result. Unless you are well trained in the defensive arts handling a group of disgruntled 'churchies' can be a tricky activity at the best of times.

Rank

Within the walls of the lodge all exterior notions of rank are removed and only those of the secret society are adhered to. This can create some problems, as many bank managers will feel more than a little miffed at having to bow before a higher ranked brother who in the outside world empties their bins. That is their problem. The hierarchy that exists in the world of the profane does not exist within your organisation.

Men of low standing in the outside world can feel worthy within your lodge but not at the expense of others. There should be no overt displays of swaggering deportment. There should be respect as well as ease and no feelings of hostility because a window cleaner is telling a chief constable where to sit.

How many levels of rank you employ is entirely up to you (see also the 33 degrees of Freemasonry). It is a question of balance. Too many and things become complicated; too few and there may be a lack of ambition and drive to climb the hierarchical structure. Remember to equate each rank with a new set of secrets or elements of your hidden agenda (if you have one).

It is also advisable, during dinners to have a '*top table*' at which the higher ranks within your society are seated, much as prefects have their separate table at school. This helps to emphasise the hierarchical situation as well as develop respect for the various offices.

Attire

You may wish to instruct your members to follow simple guidelines for behaviour when they are gathered together within the confines of the lodge. The most obvious is a dress code. Hawaiian shirts and Bermuda shorts should, in many respects, really be frowned upon unless of course you have set up your secret society in the Bahamas (such as the *Nicholl's Town Boys* or *The Cistern Point Juggers*). Smart casual is perhaps the order of the day. Some societies may frown on anything with an exterior rank badge, such as a military blazer bearing a rank of a squadron or regiment. One indeed could take offence at this because it may suggest contempt for the rules. More importantly it is a display of rank that is irrelevant to the workings of your lodge and also hints of superiority. The owner of the military blazer may in fact be lower in rank within the lodge than many in attendance and is thus displaying disrespect for others.

It is beneficial to devise some form of uniform or fancy dress for your adherents to sport while they attend lodge meetings. It is not compulsory but it is certainly wise to allow your members to dress up. They can dispense with their notions of exterior social rank and revel in the ceremonies dressed in something more suitable for their sacred position within your order. Freemasons use the apron, which grows more ornate as the various degrees are reached. They adopted this form of attire in honour of the medieval stone masons who were also the source of some of their insignias. The Knights Templar bore the now famous white tabard with its familiar red cross while the Aeolian

Brotherhood wore smocks with a cloud image over the right breast.

How you dress your members is entirely up to you but choose something fitting (no pun intended) that, in its donning, instils a sense of loyalty and the desire to progress up the ranks. Tuxedos though are recommended for dinner evenings.

Decorum

Unless you are a member of Francis Dashwood's Hellfire Club, where raucous behaviour with monkeys was encouraged, you should apply the correct standard of decorum from the start. There is no mileage in allowing free reign of uncivil rectitude to become common place. Short lived is the lodge that applies this outlook. If firm but fair rules are engaged from the start then all will be well. If you have a lax attitude initially then attempt to apply the brakes as dissension blossoms, things will certainly end in disaster. More often than not new members and indeed the more established ones are in fact looking for some form of order in their lives and therefore welcome the civility of the lodge in opposition to the unruly outside world from which they are trying to escape.

Misbehaviour should be frowned upon as a general rule with perhaps a fine levied for miscreants. The Buffaloes (RAOB) have a punitive system where for any 'swearing' other than of oaths, certain monies have to be thrown into the middle of the room. This is collected at the end of a lodge session and added to the coffers. The Aeolian

Brotherhood has similar fines for any member who lets his wind go too soon.

Any prolonged disruptive behaviour should be dealt with by ejection from your secret society with a set list and sliding scale of unwarranted activities.

Some misdemeanours:

Drinking to excess
Swearing
Defaming fellow member(s)
Bringing the lodge in disrepute
Soiling regalia
Soiling regalia of a fellow member
Misuse of the facilities
Showing off in the lodge
Showing off in public
Blowing the secrets
Blowing off in public (an Aeolian Brotherhood no-no)
Carving your initials in the Grand Master's chair
Laughing at inappropriate moments
Gurning (in all its forms)
Lewd conduct
Tardiness
Eructation
Flirting with the GM's wife on ladies' night
…and so on.

Be sure to draw up a comprehensive list and make sure they are added to your lodge handbook (given to each initiate and containing the house rules) so that members are in no doubt as to what is classed as intolerable behaviour.

The Lodge

A lodge is a place where Masons assemble and work;
hence that Assembly or duly organised society call'd a lodge,
and every Brother ought to belong to one.

Anderson's (Masonic) *Constitutions*, 1723

It's no good meeting fellow members of your organisation in a field, street corner or a car park. This will tend to dispel all the mystery that you have managed to generate and all your good work so far will come to naught. If you are going to practise fraternal fellowship then just about any property will do – obviously a more interesting building will add extra gravitas but any reasonable sized establishment will suffice. Avoid using a small flat or hiring small rooms as this restricts the workings of the lodge. Small apartments tend to be surrounded by other tenants and there's nothing worse than having a ritual initiation interrupted and ruined by a neighbour demanding that the music is too loud or that the chanting is interfering with the enjoyment of an evening's TV viewing. If you are aiming to practise the dark arts then it is recommended that a remote location would be more suitable e.g. a cave.

Some secret societies have met above public houses, inns and taverns, down in cellars and within the walls of old abandoned churches. This, in the latter example, has the added frisson of stirring up a bit of horror in the local church going community, having the knock on effect of your brotherhood gaining a dark and Satanic reputation. You may of course be tempted, depending on the style of your secret society, to choose to meet fellow initiates in an out of the way place. These venues have been made (in-) famous by the likes of the Hammer Horror films, where dark practices were carried out in the back rooms and cellars of large remote houses in the stockbroker belt or stately homes belonging to Devil worshipping second rate actors who were heavy on the ham.

Choosing the location of your lodge can be an interesting procedure and once more depends on the type of secret society you have decided to set up. On the whole lodges do tend to be 'invisible' except, for example, the Freemasons who tend to have theirs situated in very obvious places or at least not too distant from convenient car parking spaces. The one in Weston Super Mare, for example, is surrounded by high Victorian properties that look down upon it. (There is also a very obvious signpost pointing to its location.) Many Masonic halls are splendid custom-built lodges that fit a standard internal pattern and their location is not in the least secret. This kind of meeting place though may well be beyond the wallets of most. But do not worry.

There is no reason why you cannot start small and, as the membership figures increase, move on to larger premises. The stature of your lodge will directly reflect the nature of your secret society. Should you wish to use a building of status that is fine but do not rush the decision in an attempt to give your cabal an instant status it does not yet deserve. If you are choosing the anarchic/political path your lodge should be well hidden to avoid the advances of Her Majesty's constabulary and intelligence services (unless of course you have policemen in your ranks).

It is important that spouses are allowed into your lodge once, twice or several times a year. This is done to allay fears that their nearest and dearest are not up to anything untoward that may effect home life. If your secret society is an all-female affair than it's wise to let the husbands come along once in a while.

Number meeting places sequentially – the first is always Lodge number one, or the Grand Lodge. Every new one that follows must be numbered accordingly and, as stated before, can be given a name. You can if you wish levee a small fee from each meeting place in your secret society. This helps with the continual funding of your group.

The interior of your lodge can be dressed and decorated as you see fit. The prestigious use of occult symbolism is advisable. There should be the various offices, dining areas, conveniences, a kitchen and most importantly the temple or '*inner sanctum*', as it is often referred to.

Caveat: Some lodges, though, are doomed to failure, loss, degradation and to suffer all the slings and arrows of outrageous fortune. The old Golden Dawn temple in Weston Super Mare is now a building society (a non-secretive organisation). How, indeed, the mighty have fallen! If this happens rally your forces and knuckle down. The closure of one lodge does not spell disaster for all. Keep at it.

The Inner Sanctum

This is the most important room in the lodge as it is here that all the ceremonies will take place. There should be a raised area akin to a small stage or dais and there must be enough room for the assembled members to fit within this most holy of places. It is no good having to ask people to wait outside in the hall while you conduct a raising.

The inner sanctum, sometimes called the *holy of holies* or the *sanctum sanctorum*, must be the most decorated room and must give off a sense of solemn respectfulness. The ceiling must have special attention afforded it. Sometimes the zodiac is painted around a single sun at the centre. Sometimes the sun is an *All Seeing Eye* (see the reverse side of the paper currency of the United Sates) to suggest to everyone that the deity (if you have one) is watching all. Masonic lodges have the Latin words *Vide*, *Aude* and *Tace* (see, listen and be silent) usually written up high on a wall. Some lodges have seating around the inner sanctum all looking in – unless you happen to belong to the Society of Avoidance, whose members do not look at each other throughout their lodge meetings. You may also wish to add images to the floor of the temple – most Masonic lodges have the checkerboard pattern like a chessboard as their floor design.

On the stage there is usually the Grand or Worshipful Master's chair. This should be an impressive piece of ornate carpentry itself, decked out in all kinds of symbolism (relevant to your organisation). Some cushions or at least sufficient padding may be useful. A lectern or some form of table is also recommended. Candlesticks are usually found in a temple and they are well worth having for that special lighting ambience during any ceremonial event. These can either be held in tabletop candelabra or in a stand on the floor – normally around six or seven feet high.

Fees

Fees are levied so that the secret society can continue to exist. Each lodge should administer its own affairs, including raising funds, but may in accordance with your rules hand over a small percentage for the greater good. Normally each lodge acts independently, asking the Grand Lodge about matters of policy only. How much autonomy do you give? Well that may very well be reflected in whether or not you raise money by asking each lodge to contribute to the whole or if you allow them to run their own affairs without interference. This must be sorted out from the start and laid down clearly in the charter. Money is always a sticking point but lessen the problems with careful and clear thinking from the off.

Who Should Join?

Where you can you should be looking for new members from the local community. More importantly they will be like-minded individuals who are looking for something that will get them out of the house. Most, hopefully, will be looking for some additional meaning in their life beyond the links of a golf course, the office or a car showroom. Your society must offer them that.

Wealthy initiates, or rather people of a certain financial standing, are always welcome as this will aid the society in its development. Do not restrict your outlook to these individuals only but it is advisable you fill your ranks with people who can make life easier for you, as well as fellow members, in the outside world. Be vigorous with the selection process and this will pay dividends later on. Membership should be facilitated through personal invitations only. Follow this up with a home visit to see if the candidate matches your profiling system. A stable family life is always a plus.

The following is a guide as a focus for your recruitment policy:

Policemen
Solicitors and the legal profession
Doctors
Dentists
Architects
High ranking members of the Church
Her Majesty's Customs and Excise
Other secret societies (be careful!)
Hoteliers
Builders
Members of your local planning department
Company Managers (Middle management)
Entrepreneurs
Salesmen

Try to avoid:

Journalists
Members of the media
Scientists* (if your society is heavily religious)
Atheists (if your society is heavily religious)
Writers
Religious loons (if your society is scientific based)

These offer little in the way of perks and have a tendency to ask too many questions or spill the beans, although some have indeed become members of secret societies (see Esteemed Company).

*Edward Teller, the man who loved the bomb, was a Bohemian Grover but on the whole scientists will tend to wee on your fireworks.

Initiation Ceremonies

Lowliness is young ambition's ladder
Whereto the climber-upward turns his face
But when he once attains the upmost round
He then unto the ladder turns his back
Looks in the clouds scorning the base degrees
By which he did ascend...

William Shakespeare, *Julius Caesar*

In the Bard's quotation we see an all too common problem when it comes to those who have swiftly ascended the ladder of life. There is often the adoption of disdain for those with whom there was once companionship in formative years and who now stand below the initiate in rank, whether internal or external. Of course there is nothing wrong with wanting to better ourselves but we must be careful how this is attained. As in all aspects of life there are those who think nothing of using everyone and every method without so much as the commonest forms of gratitude to climb the social ladder, a trait made de rigueur in the penultimate decade of the 20th century. Unfortunately this is a fact of life and although encouraged in the outside world it is one to be frowned on within the hallowed halls of your lodge. It should not be tolerated in any form.

At any one time in your secret society there will be those who have ascended the ranks and those just joining, many of whom are desperately keen to learn all the secrets in one fell swoop, perhaps on the back of a desire to crash their way to the top and pour scorn on those below. The idea of the initiation ceremony is to keep that drive in check and maintain order and discipline. To aspire to the next level the acolyte must learn to restrain all individual motivations while they are within the bounds of the lodge, keeping about them great decorum and respect for those above and those below. This of course works at all levels of initiation throughout the 'degrees of understanding' you have decreed within your secret society. It should be encouraged so that members can transpose this beneficial behavioural idea into the outside world thus improving humanity as a whole.

Initiations, or as the Freemasons call them *raisings*, are in some respects a reward for good service to the lodge and fellow members. Depending on how you have decided to run your society, initiations may also be given after a set amount of time. You may decide that acolytes have to wait a year before they are initiated into the next level or that they have to serve every job within the lower ranks before they can be considered for 'a raise' (*a little secret society joke there*).

Ceremonies are not only employed to initiate (or raise) candidates, but they can be used for dinners, opening of a lodge session or just about anything you fancy devising a small pageant for.

Here's an example of one for opening a lodge session from the Fraternal Brotherhood of the Regency Carpets. It is merely to be considered for reference purposes only.

The assembled company wait in the ceremonial hall while the Grand Master takes his place on the dais.

Raising his arms he brings a gavel down upon a lectern (sometimes a desk). Whistling noisily he directs the company to hum along.

The whistling is commanded to stop by a secret sign.

Grand Master/Mistress: *Brothers assist me in opening the lodge. All rise!*

Everyone rises then swiftly sits down again.

Grand Master: *Are the battlements secure?* (He asks this of the person responsible for locking the doors – the Protector of the Gate.)

Protector: *They are secure from all outside intrusions.*

Grand Master: *Are the profane and their soiled manners barred from entry?*

Protector: *They are. From all intruders the doors are verily bolted. So that we may meet in peace and accord.*

Grand Master: *Are there none but us present?*

Protector: *There are none but true Carpeteers present and all be counted and obliged upon the hour.*

The Grand Master then knocks his head three times on the lectern.

Grand Master: *Will you all give the sacred sign so that we may know each other.*

The assembled then give the secret sign (anyone unable to give the sign is assumed to be an intruder and forcefully ejected or kicked in the regalia).

Warden: *The sign is given! All are true!*

The Grand Master then produces his bauble and places it in the slot.

Grand Master: *Brothers of the Carpet before the lodge is deemed open, I call upon the Great Layer of the Universe to help us this day in all our undertakings.*

The assembly then whistles inanely until gestured to stop.

Warden: *Thus verily so mote it is!*

Grand Master: *I declare then that our assembly is true. The lodge is therefore open.*

He points to all four corners of the room, the ceiling on which archaic symbols are painted (usually in garish gold) then the floor.

Grand Master: *All hail the floor!*

The floor is hailed with sharp intakes of breath.

Warden: *The kettle is on.*

Death Threats!

Freemasons will no longer have to face having their tongues cut out and their throats slit if they break their oaths. The United Grand Lodge, the society's governing body, said yesterday that it would remove references to physical penalties in candidates' obligations. The Grand Master, the Duke of Kent, has said that such references contributed to the society's reputation for secrecy and idolatry.

The Independent, June 1986

The use of death threats to secure secrecy used to be the staple of initiation ceremonies, but sadly no longer. Political correctness has seen to it that blood-curdling oaths are now no longer tolerated. In the past threats of death, dismemberment, throat cutting, the removal of one's tongue and other dire consequences were all part and parcel of the process that in the event the initiate spilled the beans he would suffer accordingly. You may wish to keep them in for effect, but with the way litigation is these days any mention of retribution may land you in the midst of an expensive court case. Threats to family and friends as a manipulative tool, employed by the more extreme ends of the underground spectrum (politico-religious, more often than not), should also be avoided.

A Typical But Generic Initiation Ceremony

"...It means a break-away from the old method and order of life..."

W. L. Wilmhurst, *The Meaning of Masonry*

An initiation ceremony can be as flamboyant or as basic as you so deem but bear in mind that the more creative and showy the ceremony the greater psychological effect it has on the initiate. Some Masonic initiations create a genuine sense of fear but as many have stated, post ceremony, it is an exhilarating and worthwhile experience nonetheless. To really hammer home the point make the '*crossing of a threshold*' a dramatic affair. Do not worry, the initiate will also feel that they have been involved in something worthwhile; that they really have given up an old way of life and have crossed over into something far more exotic and exciting. It is not enough to welcome the new member into the lodge with a handshake and a certificate. Better always to have a rousing and at the same time a *terrifying ordeal* through which the acolyte has found and stepped onto the *path of righteousness* that leads him into *enlightenment*.

The most important aspect of the initiation ceremony is to render in the initiate the most fundamental of ideas which, simply put, is that they are entering a new and brighter realm of understanding. Behind them is the old ghastly world of the profane, of chaos, ignorance and isolation out of which they are passing via the initiation ceremony into the world of light, knowledge and fellowship.

They must also understand that they will be party to profound secrets and knowledge known only to a select few. More importantly, and this must be instilled from the start, that if they reveal any of the secrets the initiate will suffer dire consequences. (See *Death Threats* above.)

The following is an initiation ceremony from the Ring Slippy Tweedians and is taken from their Book of Rough Hewn Cloth. The '**sacred**' and '**magic words**' are deliberately left out for secrecy reasons. These are taught to the candidate prior to his initiation. The single letters are the various offices throughout the order.

The candidate dressed in a hood, a lime green kaftan and red tweed slippers is brought through the double doors at the back of the lodge and is made to wait by the W. The KL coughs loudly to alert the assembled lodge.

KL: *There is an alarm at the door!*

GM: *Who seeks to be enlightened?*

GM holds up a staff and points to the star above the double doors. He utters the **sacred word**.

CANDIDATE: *Tis I, a sullen traveller on the road of stupefied ignorance. I seek* **sacred word** *in the* **sacred word** *of the* **sacred word**.

GM passes W the PT who sits down near AF until U shouts the **magic word**. GM walks swiftly towards the WSM who steps up to the podium to insert the FR into the slot on the JK. GM stands up, sits down then stands up and moves to the west whereupon the candidate steps up to the KL and offers his PN to the W.

GM walks three places to the left until he rubs up against Q before moving to stand behind W, PT and LF. Making the sacred gesture, he then moves to the first corner where he stares at the wall for a set amount of time.

W: *He is man of upstanding nature and holds his manhood firm.*

GM: *I hear.*

W: *He leaves the world behind.*

GM: *Who has brought this man?*

W: *Noble brothers. He desires to be a member, hard and true.*

GM: *All is dark.*

GM then moves to stand behind LF then takes eight steps to the left to position himself behind QR, TT and DG. He raises his staff and points to the sacred symbol directly above the candidate. The GM then takes three steps to the right and one to the left before moving across the room to stand beside the RF. He then jumps on the spot for five counts before heading to the second corner.

GM: *Darkness surrounds the brother to be.*

The hood is double-checked by the TG and the W.

W: *Upon this hour it is so done that this brother who walks in darkness, awaits rebirth into light. The binds that bind him are born of ignorance and fear.*

The W places a noose of string around the candidate's neck and ties a knot. The GM hops once while the GH, the TF and RP lurch randomly backwards and forwards. GM says the **magic word** then returns to the lectern and coughs three times to alert the assembled that he is about to make utterances.

GM: *Brothers, we have in our midst a man in darkness. He lives in peril.*

W: *Speak candidate!*

CANDIDATE: *Tis I. The lost one. Ignorance of things Tweed.*

The GM begins jumping on the spot for five counts then squats. Raising his hands to the sacred symbol above he winks at the GR who moves to stand beside the WT who, on taken this cue, shuffles across the room to stand by the W. The RP, GH, TF and the QR form a rank, take a step forward then lean backwards.

The assembled then each remove a slipper.

GM: *In honour of this man's admission we make the first sign.*

The first sign is made.
The second sign is made followed by the fifth.
The second sign is made followed by the fifth, the eight and the tenth. This is then followed by the second and first again.

W: *The signs are given that we may recognise.*

The GM then rushes to the third corner where he faces the wall.

GM: *This brother in darkness wishes to be considered a wearer of tweed.*

KL: *Tis so. The sun riseth and the sun sinketh but we wear the tweed.*

GM: *By his acceptance he will be taught the ancient mysteries.*

Everyone falls down then gets up after a count of three.

The GM then returns to the lectern and raises his hands high above his head. The WSM makes a mess then gathers together the rolls of tweed from their place of storage. The GM turns his back and cups his hands over his ears.

Three ensconced candles are lit, extinguished, then re-lit.

The W, RP, GH, TF and the KL exchange places then form a cordon around the candidate. They point at the candidate. The W steps forward and 'comforts' the candidate to a kneeling position.

The GM then moves to stand in front of the candidate holding a sword to the man's breast. The W whoops once, then twice then whistles one continuous note for the count of 20. GM then instructs the candidate to lean forward.

GM: *This is the sword of Jeraboam.*

The assembled give the third sign and utter the **sacred word**. Followed by the **magic word**, said twice.

GM hops on one foot then rushes to the fourth corner. The sword will still be against the candidate's breast but is now held by the W.

GM: *The sword sits in judgement of your ability.*

ALL: *All hail the sword!*

GM: *Candidate, do you understand that to reveal what you learn will mean?*

ALL: *All extremities removed by force!*

CANDIDATE: *I do. I do solemnly swear that I am to the task.*

GM: *Bring him unto light!*

W: *Unto light we bring him!*

The hood is removed with one dramatic gesture. Everyone runs around then stops at the count of three. Sweets are then handed around and everyone is happy. GM remains in the corner until the lodge closing ceremony at the end of the evening's festivities.

This is just one example of an initiation ceremony. You can make yours as elaborate or as simple as you so desire. The more elaborate the ritual – the greater the psychological effect, making the acolyte feel as if they have really been through the initiation process mill. Simply handing over an apron or a sash is not the done thing. You must make them feel as if they have really crossed over a threshold or entered into something really special. In short, lay it on thick!

In Alexander Piatigorsky's *Who's Afraid of the Freemasons?* there are 30 pages or so of Masonic rituals for you to consult for additional ideas.

Degrees and Levels of Initiation

You must decide how many levels there are within your secret society. Each level must improve on the last in terms of the secrets revealed and the method of passing from one level to the next through a particular ceremony. Each of these rituals must convince the acolyte that they are going to be a little further down the road to understanding the greater mysteries that you have been hinting at since day one. More importantly each ritual must be more impressive than the last.

As the candidates have passed from the outside world to the new life of a member of your group they are in fact still very much *in the dark* when it comes to what is really going on. Each successive 'raising' to the next level brings *more light* upon them. It is in a sense a gradual transition as opposed to an instant one.

It is recommended that a Super Grand Master (or a name of your choosing) must be positioned at the highest degree attainable in your organisation. He must have moved up through the ranks and must know all the ceremonies and ritualistic words off by heart. He, or indeed she, must also be able to perform all rituals without slip or error.

The 33 Degrees of Freemasonry

Lowest at the top.

1. Entered Apprentice
2. Fellow Craft
3. Master Mason

---

4. Secret Master
5. Perfect Master
6. Intimate Secretary
7. Provost and Judge
8. Intendant of the Building
9. Elect of Nine
10. Elect of 15
11. Sublime Elect
12. Grand Master Architect

13. Royal Arch (of Enoch)
14. Scottish Knight of Perfection
15. Knight of the Sword or of the East
16. Prince of Jerusalem
17. Knight of the East and West
18. Knight of the Pelican and Eagle and Sovereign Prince Rose Croix of Heredom
19. Grand Pontiff
20. Venerable Grand Master
21. Patriarch Noachite
22. Prince of Libanus
23. Chief of the Tabernacle
24. Prince of the Tabernacle
25. Knight of the Brazen Serpent
26. Prince of Mercy
27. Commander of the Temple
28. Knight of the Sun
29. Knight of St Andrew
30. Grand Elected Knight Kadosh, Knight of the Black and White Eagle
31. Grand Inspector Inquisitor Commander
32. Sublime Prince of the Royal Secret
33. Grand Inspector General

You will probably not need as many as 33. You may wish to think about levels of initiation that relate to particular numbers – seven, nine and thirteen are all numbers imbued with some form of magical significance. You will find most numbers have some special meaning to someone some-where. So take your pick.

Coded Messages, Signals and Glyphs

It is often necessary to communicate with fellow secret society members at the national or international level.

It is sometimes worthwhile testing the water when it comes to applying for a job, discussing matters with the bank or any other normal day to day environment, to see if a fellow member is able to assist. With the careful use of code words or rather to put it a better way *'recognition'* words, great personal benefit can be found within the walls of the workplace.

Signals are another sure-fire way of alerting a potential ally to your allegiances. They should take the form of discreet gestures that could almost be mistaken for normal activities, such as scratching the nose or wiping fluff from a jacket. Touching the forehead, running your fingers along your lapel, putting a finger up a nostril, scratching a part of the body (avoid the groin), the position of crossed legs – can all be used as secret gestures for a mute, clandestine conversation.

Just a few 'signals' you may wish to consider devising:

Secrecy
Saying hello
Distress
Fidelity
Put that away
Level of initiation
Whoops
Fancy a pint

Yes

No

Pardon

Not just now

Can you tell me where the nearest lodge is please?

A one off signal needs to be backed up with a confirmation. A single gesture may be misinterpreted so employ a sequence that leaves the recipient in no doubt as to who you are.

It is often suggested that fellow members of a secret society are there to aid their fellows as a sign of mutual dependence and to encourage a sense of brotherhood. The world can be a desperate and difficult place and any victory great or small that can ease the way is always welcome.

Here's an example. Running and owning a car is an expensive duty, particularly when it comes to repairs – especially those on luxury vehicles (when on the rare occasions they do break down, of course). How much better it would be to have a fellow society member who is a garage mechanic who would be able to cut costs and treat you with the respect you deserve, instead of some rude unwashed youth who works for a company ready to overcharge you for inspecting your sills. Using a secret foot position or a hand gesture may alert a garage employee that you share a brotherhood. By recognising your subtle movements, he will afford you due consideration.

Of course in any one town you may already know all the members of your society so recognition signs and coded words become more beneficial when travelling around the country or abroad.

A series of distress signals may be of benefit as well. In the unlikely event you are in court or have just been arrested a '*gestured indication*' of your allegiance may work in your favour.

Glyphs, small images or motifs, are really useful and can be used to alert fellow members of your cabal as to what's going on or that you are a noble fellow Brother, especially in written correspondences. Glyphs can be incorporated into documents, graffiti or lodge and regalia adornments.

Getting to Grips

You may wish to utilise special handshakes, known as *grips*, in the secret society business. Not all organisations use them but they are worth having. The grips usually signify which level of initiation the member is at. Thus a second level member for example will able to tell when gripped properly which level the stranger before him has achieved. Sometimes a grip might not be recognised or may be missed. The subtle use of additional telltale signs will allow the social intercourse to function smoothly and without confusion. You can spend several satisfying hours trying out different hand positions to find the ones that best suit you and your brotherhood.

Passwords

We are all familiar with the passwords employed by school age gangs, troops and clubs so that admission can be refused to suspicious characters. Passwords, or '*Shibboleths*' as they are sometimes called, can be a single word that can be dropped into conversation to alert anyone in the room as to your secret affiliations or can be used to gain entry to a lodge or lodges particularly those out of town or in unfamiliar territory. They are called Shibboleths because when Jephthah, of the Gileadites, caught the fleeing Ephraimites, he asked each captive to say the word shibboleth, which means '*a stream in flood*'. The fugitives could not pronounce the word properly because they could not create the 'sh' sound (Judges 16: 1–16)

Entry to a lodge may require a sequence of passwords or indeed whole sentences and correct responses that have to be learnt by heart. This avoids a lucky chance use of a password (often the staple of naff films) that the person desiring entry may happen upon. It is advisable to follow this latter course and have a long sequence of passwords in the form of a structured 'conversation', including secret words known only to your secret society. The following is just a brief section from the *Lodge Appeal* of the Ring Slippy Tweedians.

Warden: Hail.

Person at door: Hail.

Warden: Quid -?

Person at door: Pro Quo.

Warden: Give me that word.

Person at door: The word is true and long and difficult to spell.

Warden: As it is to all men.

Person at door: But all men are not as I…

Remember to devise something that is relatively short in duration. If it is too long the lodge meeting will be over before everyone is in. The Roundhouse Boys had a series of passwords for entry to their lodge that took one hour and twenty-six minutes, while the Elusive Order of Social Mysfits had an entry to the lodge ceremony that was just over a month long.

Person at door: Knock, knock.

Warden: Who's there

Person at door: Caesar.

Warden: Caesar who?

Person at door: Caesar firmly from behind and Rome around up front.

That exchange was from the Loyal Brethren of the Stinking Frond. It is of course funnier in the original cod Latin.

Salutator: Pulsus, pulsus.

Praefectus: Quis est libi?

Salutator: Caesar.

Praefectus: Excrementum!

In contrast the Nude Lads had a single word to gain entry to their lodges, the word was '*ummm?*'

Written Correspondence

When you are writing a letter or engaging in some form of written correspondence it is beneficial to drop subtle hints (other than glyphs) about who you are just in case the recipient of your screed is a fellow member of your secret society. Obviously this will not be the case in the early years but as your group expands across the country, and if you are blessed, across the world, you will need to communicate with them without revealing too much to a third party who may happen upon your letter.

The rule of thumb is nothing too overt. Do not be tempted to use such terms as '*Worshipful Master*', '*lodge brother*', '*as a fellow member of...*' Subtlety is the order of the day.

Selecting identifying code words from your initiation ceremony might be a useful ploy but just one word only – one that perhaps has two meanings, an everyday normal use and one that can also be interpreted as being part of your secret society. *Savaloy* might be too obscure or misconstrued, whereas *civility* fits the bill perfectly.

Sign the letter as per normal but maybe add a 'lodge' number after the name or more interestingly hyphenate your name with that of your meeting house. If for example your name is *Bernard Goole* who attends the *Corinthian* lodge, add '*Corinthian*' so that your name becomes '*Bernard Goole-Corinthian*'. Fellow members of your society who know that lodges are called Corinthians will know exactly where your allegiances lie.

You may also employ the use of other hints within the text as indicators of who you are, such as a double hyphen, four full stops and double commas. Hours of fun can be had coming up with special sigils for your society's use.

Secret Alphabet

This is not an absolute must, but an idea worth considering. It is a time consuming, but worthwhile, endeavour. Of late, secret alphabets have lost much of their gilt and, indeed, usefulness. Secret alphabets should perhaps only be employed for the more anarchic cabals but feel free to use one if you wish.

Secret alphabets are something very much from the past but are charming nonetheless. You can draw one up to add a sense of history, making claims that it was once used, centuries before, but is now redundant. A secret alphabet can be a useful tool in the construction of your secret society's back-story.

The modern Rosicrucians or AMORC (not to be confused with the original and in all likelihood bogus secret society from the 17th century) use one based on triangles similar in many respects to that employed by the Knights Templar – which was based on positions in a Templar cross.

Cryptography

For more interesting and exciting times it can be fun to use secret codes and other old standby tricks such as invisible ink. Use of these on the whole is limited to the more clandestine, anarchic and revolutionary organisations. Though one can have great fun sending out dinner invites as codes. Most methods have been around for centuries stretching back as far as ancient cultures. Most ciphers are now 'crackable', unless, of course, you have a supercomputer such as the Cray as an asset of your secret society.

Research the following methods:

1. Invisible ink
2. Use of superfluous words
3. Misplaced words
4. Vertical and diagonal reading
5. Artificial word groupings
6. Stencil plates
7. Using two letters (Bacon's Cipher)
8. Transposition of letters
9. Letter substitution
10. Counterpart tabulations
11. Mixed symbols – dots, lines, crosses
12. Printed key and code book

13. Use of number substitutes or numerals

The delightfully named Mr Thicknesse, an 18th-century expert in such matters, came up with a method employing musical notation to code messages. Great pleasure can be gained from creating your own codes, ciphers and methods of transmitting secret messages. As email and the Internet are open to abuse and surveillance by the authorities, it is perhaps time for the hand-written code to make a come back.

Bad Eggs

Any organisation will have its bad eggs. It is a fact of life. Undoubtedly you will initiate someone into your society only to discover that they are rotten to the core or that they are exploiting their position to the detriment of everyone involved. How you deal with them is entirely down to you, but they must be ejected immediately. Bad eggs have brought trouble and strife to numerous secret societies throughout the ages. One only has to look at the activities of P2, an Italian Masonic lodge, to see the consequences. The Freemasons acted quickly to distance themselves from the rogue elements and dispensed their retribution in a swift manner. You must do likewise. Brook no bad behaviour.

It is wise to associate yourself with the book *How to Remove Soiled Members* by Richard Prills.

We did strip him of his badges and after some rumination removed his baubles, his pantaloons of office, his quin, his smunt, his fresbel and his hoodad… For he had brought shame upon the Brotherhood of the Frilly Adventures. No more would he flick his potatoes to the detriment of all.

Richard Prills,
Lodge Attendant,
Brotherhood of The Frilly Adventures, 1867

In Times of Hot Water

In times of overt political hoohah you may have to take your secret society deep 'underground' in an act that is certainly no metaphor. Dictatorships, religious intolerance and social paranoia have all contributed over the centuries to an adverse publicity when it comes to the public understanding of just what it is secret societies are attempting.

It can be a real rollercoaster at times. Take this Russian example from the 18th century onward…

Under Catherine the Great of Russia, Freemasonry blossomed. Some Masons were arrested though for 'revolutionary' activity, which turned out on the whole to be nothing more than a few moans in the odd book or two. Paul I did his best to suppress Freemasonry but attempted no outright ban. Then it was okay again when Alexander I took up the reins (he was a Mason). Then in 1822, it all kicked off again when he decided to stamp out all secret societies (boo!). By 1825 all Freemasonry had been banned, so Russian Freemasons all became members of foreign lodges, particularly French ones. By 1906 it was all back on again.

This is just one example of what you may come across, but be prepared for such eventualities. Society at large is a fickle beast at best, as is public opinion. Take nothing for granted and be prepared for the absolute worst. People's opinion about you will change like the tides.

Here is another famous example, often cited, in which the French newspaper *Le Moniteur* showed its readers how to shift opinion concerning Napoleon. 'The *brigand* flees from the island of Elba'; the *usurper* arrives at Grenoble'; '*Napoleon* enters Lyons'; ' The *Emperor* reaches Paris this evening.'

Dealing with Political Intrigue

Secret societies and political intrigue go hand in hand. Sometimes the conspiracy theorists do get it right – they simply muddle their thinking. Most accusations of manipulation have their roots not in world domination, but in the acquisition of power for accruing wealth. It is the most basic and destructive urge that humanity is prone to. In many of the more recent scandals involving secret societies it is the vast amounts of money being made and laundered through various financial institutions that garners rabid media interest.

On the whole your members at a grass roots level will not be involved with anything on that level. Frankly, powerful people have to mix with other powerful people to pull off stunts like international banking fraud. It will take time and effort to reach those dizzying heights, so put it off your wish list for now.

If a member of your cadre is caught with his hand in the till, the media and conspiracy theorists will be swift in their condemnation of your organisation as a whole. They will state that it is proof that you and your fellow members are out to line your pockets at the expense of society. They will follow this with accusations of undemocratic and anti-social behaviour. More devastatingly they will demand the banning of your secret society.

In short, leave political manipulation to those who can. Avoid involving yourself with such activities until you are confident enough that there are initiates in high places who can cover your tracks.

Be warned that other groups may wish to discredit you or simply blame you for some scandalous situation that has broken upon the public consciousness. You may find your organisation has become nothing more than a useful scape-goat. There will always be a backlash to secrecy but do not feel you have to come out and defend yourself, particularly if others drop you in it. Sometimes there is strength in silence. By neither confirming nor denying you will add a welcome gravitas to your activities. All publicity is good publicity, even the bad.

Distaff

It is very easy to assume that secret societies are predominantly a preserve of the male and that they suffer a men-only bias. Not so. There is nothing to stop the development of female-only secret societies. The Freemasons have women-only lodges, so if they can do it, you certainly can.

There are no special requirements per se for distaff lodges and how they run their affairs is entirely up to them.

This is still very much a man's world, so for that extra element of spice a women-only secret society is bound to really put the wind up some old creaking male elements of the establishment.

There is a dreadful sexist joke that says women have never undertaken this kind of activity because they cannot keep a secret for more than five minutes. Turn that cliché on its head. Prove to your detractors that you can be as powerful and influential as your male counterparts.

In the 18th century the Hon. Elizabeth St. Leger, daughter of Lord Doneraile, was initiated into the Freemasons after hiding herself in an empty clock case. She witnessed the activities of her father's lodge and the only way they could swear her to secrecy was to initiate her into the Brotherhood. If there had been an established ladies-only secret society at the time Liz would not have bothered spying on her dad. The Odd Fellows allow women, but their once secret (or rather semi-secret) status has long fallen by the wayside. There are 30 sororities in the American college system, perhaps proving the idea that female 'societies' are more prevalent across the pond.

III

In Which Sundries are Discussed.

For words, like Nature, half reveal
And half conceal the Soul within…

Tennyson, *In Memoriam*

Should You Make Them Worried?

As you go about your secret society business you will doubtless become worried about the hysterical reactions of extremists who blame secret societies for all their woes. They will perceive a threat where there is (apparently) none, but will want to use this supposed threat as an excuse for political manipulation in waves of brow-beating hysteria.

As already stated, we live in a period where fear is used as a powerful socio-political tool – fear of the outsider, the asylum seeker, the terror suspect. These are all phrases that have had their meanings subverted, a process of '*enemification*', to use an invented Rumsfeldism (he may not have used this word, but it is one he would have eventually come up with!). Conspiracy theorists are equally guilty of using this fear, as is the Church who continue to demonise secret societies for fear of losing ground to freethinkers and radicals who are often cheesed off with the religious hypocrisy of papal doctrine (such as Francis Dashwood). Minority groups are demonised throughout the world – they're useful whipping boys for all of society's ills and a good way for the powers-that-be to distract critics from their own failings. The same way certain reactionary reporters on the right like to blame liberals and atheists for the state of the world. Or the left moaning about greedy 'fat cat' industrialists plundering the world's resources. Everybody wants to blame someone else for the way things are.

You should endeavour to remain calm and circumspect. Trying to counter these claims will bring you into direct conflict with your accusers. It is tempting, and indeed correct, to give your critics their just desserts but in the realm of the secret society it is safer and nobler to remain above the fuss.

It is recommended that you make subtle efforts to remind people to worry about more important issues, such as fundamentalist religion in all its hues with its attendant anti-science rather than inventing conspiratorial global domination agendas. We continue to live in a non-secular world. The Dark Age continues. The comfort of myths are more important than scientific reality. Suggest to your critics that they should really concern their thoughts with pseudo-science, political extremists, failing resources and the environment. Have them worry about greedy banks and companies who will not be happy until every square inch of the planet is sold for a high profit.

Note: If your cabal is involved in oil exploitation and resource grabbing you may wish to remain totally off the radar and/or ignore some of the above.

What to Look For in Conspiracy Theorists

Understanding the 'conspiracy theorist' can lead to some rewarding publicity. By understanding how they think and operate you can add a genuine frisson of sinister activity to your secret society by playing up their fears.

For the conspiratorialist, all manner of demonic forces have been at work throughout history, including of course, the Jews, but also the Illuminati, Knights Templar, Knights of Malta, Masons, Freemasons, Cosmopolitans, Abolitionists, Slaveholders, Catholics, Communists, Council on Foreign Relations, Trilateral Commission, Warren Commission, World Wildlife Fund, International Monetary Fund, League of Nations, United Nations and many more...

Michael Shermer, *Why People Believe Weird Things*

Excellent! Your ambition should be to get on that list. Remember as well that incompetence is often mistaken as conspiracy so be careful what you deem as such.

Conspiracy theorists have this patronising idea that we are all zombies – that we somehow fail to see what's going on in the world. They like to lecture us about how asleep we are or that the Devil's having his wicked way with our souls. It is without doubt nothing but a heady concoction of delusion to make them feel self-important and that what they have to say is somehow relevant to us all – a process of self-grandisement. Ask yourself: are Freemasons really going to tell a billion Muslims, the Chinese or the Roman Catholic Church what to do? Of course not. For you, it does not matter what those who entertain paranoid delusions think but once they turn their attentions on you, look out! Knowing how your enemy operates can really be a positive boon and will certainly put you on the map if a conspiracy theorist gets wind of your activities, especially if you play up to their fears and wild imaginings. Have a go! You may be surprised at the outcome.

Most of these people operate under a Messiah complex, believing that they are the only ones who can save us or defend us from the great threat. More often than not they are paranoid Christians who see the Devil attending to his nefarious work through the channel of a secret society. One conspiracy theorist even committed suicide with the sole intention of trying to make his death look like a suspicious murder so that his fears about shadow forces would be justified to the outside world.

Some even make the silly statement that microchips are going to be inserted into our heads. Just how much is that going to cost? How much to run the computer systems that would control us? My computer at home is always crashing as I am sure yours does – imagine a system that controls six billion people! What if it succumbs to a virus? You'll have to reboot all the people in the high street. Not very likely is it?

These people are very keen to trivialise all history into being nothing more than the machinations of secret societies, usually atheistic, Jewish and/or left wing. This is simply patronising and very stupid. These people would have us believe that revolutions must be the work of underground cadres because the great unwashed are not capable of thinking for themselves. Humanitarianism, freedom and the throwing off of religious persecution must surely be the result of atheistic secret societies, because the peasants can hardly think for themselves. Well, they can.

In their book *Nazis, Communists, Klansmen, and Others on the Fringe: Political Extremism in America*, John George and Laird Wilcox outlined a useful set of characteristics to look for in conspiracy theorists. By knowing these you will able to focus your attentions on creating a mythology around your cabal. It will certainly help bring attention to your secret society if you know what conspiratorial buttons to press as part of your PR campaign.

1. Absolute certainty they have the truth.
2. America (*or insert country of choice*) is controlled to a greater or lesser extent by a conspiratorial group. In fact, they believe this evil group is very powerful and controls most nations.
3. Open hatred of opponents. Because these opponents (actually 'enemies' in the extremists' eyes) are seen as part of or sympathisers with 'The Conspiracy', they deserve hatred and contempt.
4. Little faith in the democratic process. Mainly because most believe 'The Conspiracy' has such influence in the US government (or wherever), and therefore extremists usually spurn compromise.
5. Willingness to deny basic civil liberties to certain fellow citizens, because enemies deserve no liberties.
6. Consistent indulgence in irresponsible accusations and character assassination.

This list was focused on Holocaust deniers in the book, but it works equally well for any of the unhinged conspiracy '*the truth is out there: I want to believe*' type theorists with too much time on their hands. As a rough guide to how these people think have a look at the adverts that appear in psychic magazines or those periodicals dealing with the more bizarre and outré. There will be no end of relationship related premium rate help lines, ads for weapons, surviving alien abduction memorabilia and gentlemen only Internet sites.

What They Believe

"Okay, here's what we've got: The Rand Corporation, in conjunction with the saucer people, under the supervision of the reverse vampires, are forcing our parents to go to bed early in a fiendish plot to eliminate the meal of dinner... We're through the looking glass here, people..."

Milhouse, *The Simpsons*

Here is a brief selection of conspiracy theories that secret societies are said to be involved in. Those claimed to be responsible are in brackets. Notice how many times the Freemasons appear. It must be carefully noted that those said to be behind such events will vary depending on who has concocted the theory. Sometimes the machinations are undertaken by secret societies working in tandem, under the control of or in conflict with another cadre. As an exercise, try and fit your group into one of the following:

The whole of Earth's history. (*All of them*)
Trade Centre attacks of September 11 2001. (*Freemasons, Illuminati, Templars, Bohemian Grove, Bilderberg, Skull and Bones, Knights of Malta*)
The JFK assassination. (*Freemasons, Bohemian Grove, Templars, Illuminati, Bilderberg, Mafia, Minutemen*)
The (non-) moon landings. (*Freemasons, Nazis*)
Secret moon bases. (*Freemasons, Nazis*)
The French Revolution. (*Freemasons*)
The Russian Revolution. (*Freemasons*)

132

Anything to do with Jesus Christ (aka Joshua Ben Joseph). (*All of them*)

The Holy Grail (whatever that is). (*All of them*)

ID Cards (UK). (*Freemasons, Illuminati, Bohemian Grove, Bilderberg*)

Fluoride in drinking water. (*Freemasons*)

The formation of the United States. (*Freemasons*)

E numbers in food. (*Freemasons*)

Toothpaste (don't ask!). (*Freemasons*)

Dropping the atomic bombs on Japan. (*Freemasons, Illuminati, Templars, Bohemian Grove, Skull and Bones*)

Pearl Harbor. (*Freemasons, Bohemian Grove, Illuminati, Templars, Skull and Bones*)

The Death of Calvi – 'God's Banker'. (*Freemasons, P2, Mafia, Opus Dei*)

Challenger shuttle disaster. (*Freemasons, Nazis, Skull and Bones*)

Area 51. (*Freemasons, Bohemian Grove, Illuminati, Nazis, Skull and Bones*)

Fall of the Berlin Wall. (*Freemasons, Bilderberg, Bohemian Grove, Skull and Bones*)

Invasion of Iraq × 2. (*Freemasons, Lions, Rotarians, Bohemian Grove, Bilderberg, Templars, Opus Dei, Skull and Bones*)

Crop circles. (*Templars, Freemasons, aliens in alliance with…*)

Chupacabras. (*Freemasons, Skull and Bones, Illuminati, aliens in alliance with…*)

By aligning yourself with a conspiracy it will increase your chances of gaining that sought after reputation which can enhance your standing no end. Clambering onto the conspiracy theory bandwagon is a sure-fire way of becoming noticed and shaking off general indifference. But be selective as to which one you embrace.

The greatest hurdle you will face when setting up your secret society will be avoiding any attention from those overly keen to label you with the epithet 'cult'. In order to counter their finger pointing a brief description of the make up of a cult is outlined next.

Cults

"I'm not the Messiah!"

*"I say you are, my Lord, and I should know,
I've followed a few..."*

Monty Python's *The Life of Brian*

The worlds of cults, secret societies and religion often overlap in something not dissimilar to a Venn diagram. Religion can often be the source of a cult and vice versa, but not always. Cults do have many characteristics that are overtly religious. The following is included for research purposes in that, by avoiding the pitfalls of cultish behaviour, you will be able to steer your clandestine ship free from the lagoons and reefs of misunderstanding.

Cults on the whole occupy the territory that exists somewhere between a secret society and a religion. Both are seen within the make up and structure of these entities and often share similarities to both. Cults, on the whole, tend to be off-shoots of religion, where a disaffected adherent decides that the tenets of faith do not come up to scratch against their own highly personal view of what that religion should be and decides to create a belief system in their own likeness. It has often been said, indeed oft quoted, that the quickest way to make money is to form a religion! What is a religion other than a well-developed cult? L. Ron Hubbard is the most famous proponent of this idea. He developed (started on a bet and a flip of a coin) the cult religion Dianetics or, as it's more commonly known, Scientology.

Usually the spin-off cult contains a mixture of plundered religious material from a number of sources, not necessarily those with a Christian slant, and is often a hybrid concoction of mumbo jumbo from a variety of diverse credos. Buddhist thought can often be found hand-in-hand with Judaism, Satanism and, on occasions, Freemasonry (as ever).

Cults on the whole tend to be more ephemeral than either religions or secret societies. There are of course exceptions to this rule in the form of say Christianity which started off as a cult or Hare Krishna (The International Society For Krishna Consciousness) which only began in the 1960s, but has survived well beyond the average lifespan of similar organisations. Again Scientology is another example of a long-lived cult, one beloved of numerous film stars, which undoubtedly adds to its mystique and its survival despite its bogus claims of our alien ancestry. Another example of a long-lived cult would be Mormonism or the Church of Latter Day Saints, dreamt up by Joseph Smith in 1830 after his supposed encounter with an angel named Moroni.

Cults are always focused around a charismatic and deeply psychotic leader – for example the 'Rev' Jim Jones of the People's Temple made infamous by the mass suicides in Gayana in South America. This cult leader is someone who is troubled mentally, suffering delusions of grandeur born of an unhappy or at the least a troubled childhood (including bullying, toy burning, bed wetting). That perhaps is too simplistic a psychological reason as there are undoubtedly numerous facets that go to make up the mindset of a cult leader. But the evidence tends to favour a fractured and disjointed upbringing. Charles Manson – one time 'most dangerous man in America' – was the son of a teenage prostitute and spent many years in and out of various correctional facilities before starting his notorious activities.

De rigueur for the cult is the notion that the charismatic leader has convinced themselves, and of course their followers, that they are the second coming of Christ or in the case of the Satanic cults, the Devil himself. Through them the faithful will be saved while the rest of the ungodly world will be cast into Hell or other similar bombastic fire and brimstone infernos. This has obvious parallels with religions and with some secret societies. The cult is formed for the sole purpose of gratification of the charismatic leader who, perhaps lacking attention and love, demands it by force and manipulation from those he or she dupes into following them. In many cases, the cult members are there just to act out the cult leader's paranoid fantasies focused around one or more of the usual suspects: Jews, One World Government, Satan, Communists and so on. Parallels exist here with the more extremist conspiracy theorists who seek to lay blame for their own failings in the so-called machinations of back room cadres.

There is always a strong sexual element in the more charismatic, often bloodthirsty cults born perhaps of the leader's inability to form anything like a serious relationship with anyone in the past. Sometimes the cult leader is just after the high life and extorts money from cult members. He or she is simply out to line his or her pockets to revel in great wealth, while their unquestioning subjects drift about in sandals and saris believing their leader is all powerful, all knowing and deserving of an opulent lifestyle. There are of course obvious parallels here with the hellfire and damnation TV evangelists and preachers prevalent on US television or certain Swamis in India and the West Coast of the United States.

Cult members themselves are usually of a surprisingly stable nature, at least at first. It is claimed that they are the victims of guile, cunning and devious psychological techniques. How else could seemingly normal, middle class, well educated individuals fall for the nonsense that makes up the teachings of all cults? Interestingly enough the real reasons for cult membership are not always that clear cut and our social backgrounds are no defence. We are after all human and whatever our social standing we all fall prey to weasel words and social manipulation through the prestigious misuse of psychology. Banks, politicians, television commercials and salesman for example all employ the same methods as cult leaders and religions to win us over. We resist yet still we succumb. However clever we think we are.

The existence of cults says more about society, perhaps, than any one charismatic leader. Cults reflect, as do religions and other belief systems, a quest for meaning in life. As science pushes back the boundaries of our understanding of the universe all of our old ideas rapidly become redundant. For example, humanity's unique position at the centre of a god's creation is now nothing more than a ridiculous and outdated concept. We live in a small planet around a less than average star out on the edge of an ordinary galaxy, which is one of a hundred billion in the known universe. We are not special in any way. We feel vulnerable. Lost. Cults and religions step in to offer succour.

In the face of this awesome knowledge we are humbled. Many do not like the fact that science has removed the mythical make-believe entity as a cause of 'creation'. In an odd twist of religio-logic science is said to be nothing but the work of the Devil. Many cult leaders despise science; some steal the word and use it to give their cadre a more acceptable face, for example the School of Economic Science (not to be confused with the London School of Economics – although some would argue otherwise), which is nothing more than a sham concoction of nonsensical philosophies. Or Christian Science, which is about as oxymoronic a statement as it is possible to get.

But all the blame for cult membership cannot be laid solely at the feet of so called Messiahs, however charismatic they are. It is a two way street. Too many people are ready to accept the nonsense that greets them daily without question (newspapers are full of it). Many perhaps are on a quest to find meaning having failed to find it in the mainstream religions. Some are kicking out against repressive ideologies, consumerism, or a stifling home life. Sometimes new cult members are suffering mental health problems, are homeless, or are drug addicts or social misfits and loners desperate for sympathy and a solid base – somewhere they can call home.

There is also the same socio-psychological need at work best displayed with the desire to become part of a select elite, from secret societies through to golf club membership.

All play on the notion of special status. Despite the persistent use of the buzz word 'individuality', continually pumped into the population via adverts and the like, humans are gregarious and need the company and fellowship of like-minded people. As already stated, television advertising is just as guilty of using coercion techniques as the cults that society so desperately fears. Politicians and political parties employ the same processes as cults do. At the moment fear is the most powerful tool at their disposal. To combat that fear all of us must be prepared to question that which is presented to us.

Cults have a tangential influence on politics in respect to policy. At best they will influence the legal system and police methodology in respect to control and prosecution but rarely influence governments unless they grow to a scale that parallels organised religion. The best example of this would be the Church of Latter Day Saints or Mormons – a cult that has done very well indeed and one that does have a major influence on US government systems, particularly at the grass roots level.

But politics itself is not immune from the ideas and tenets of cult behaviour. In North Korea, for example, the political system is in effect one large cult with the reverence laid before the 'Dear Leader' whose will is immutable. This is a cult writ large ensnaring a whole nation to the point of subservience. The inability to question any policy laid before the populace becomes ingrained.

In many respects political extremist ideologies are cults. Hitler's National Socialism being a prime example with its perverse ideologies, crass mythic elements, daft pseudo-science and fevered ignorance enabling the Nazis to ensnare nearly a whole nation, as well as others, even today, in its sway. It was not a secular state, as some Christians would have it. German soldiers had '*God with Us*' (in German of course) on their belt buckles!

The National Socialist party did not tolerate secret societies, because it was itself a secret society, with its grand master, its racist gnosis, its rites and initiations.

Rene Alleau
Les Sources Occultes du Nazisme,
Paris, Grasset, 1969

The Führer was venerated with deference and without question, his will was all and anyone who fell beyond the boundaries of thought and the confines of Nazism was considered a traitor and was duly punished in the extreme. Hitler himself thought he was on some divine path, that he was a Messiah, chosen to lead his 'people' to some glorious future and that the Germans, or rather Aryans, were the special people – the Ubermensch. Pre-World War Two Germany had numerous secret societies and cults related to paganism, anti-Semitism and 'back to the soil' neo-Nazi fraternities who romanticised Teutonic ideals.

The same could also be said of Stalin – a cult of personality – that of 'Uncle Joe,' held millions in the thrall of yet more perverse ideologies this time from the other end of the political swingometer. In reality who can tell the difference between these two extremes? Millions were slaughtered for cult-like messiahs and beliefs. Deluded extremism is a dangerous thing wherever it exists.

Blame the 1960s!

The strident political Right are very taken with the idea of blaming the 1960s for all manner of social ills, from single mothers and social breakdown to a lack of respect for authority. They are desperately wrong, of course, but one fall out of the *Tune In, Turn On and Drop Out* generation was the idea of the quick-fix and the rise of the Guru who, seeing that the young were throwing off the shackles of their parents in search of a better life, decided that creating faux religions with daft ideologies was the best way to make a fast buck.

In the quest for new meaning in the world critical thought was pushed aside allowing a free for all, anything goes mentality which was just as destructive as the 'old ways' the young were trying to rid themselves of. Minds were happy to accept any glamorous nonsense that promised great revelations. True, that is not something that is purely a 1960s phenomenon – it is prevalent throughout human history.

What made the 1960s interesting in this respect was that science and technology were making great leaps forward while simultaneously there was still a widespread profusion of a 'Middle Ages' mentality. Nothing changes, I hear you say. While we were busy sending man into space a whole gamut of nonsensical mindsets were in the ascendance. True, it is wise in hindsight to be dismissive of these new ideas but at the time a sea change was happening and in one respect that was a positive step forward. At least questions were being asked about the nature of reality. It was simply that they came up with bogus answers from looking entirely in the wrong places.

But there is a fine balance between mindless acceptance and outright hard line scepticism. As Carl Sagan said in his 1987 Pasadena lecture The Burden of Scepticism: '*It seems to me what is called for is an exquisite balance between two conflicting needs: the most sceptical scrutiny of all hypotheses that are served up to us and at the same time a great openness to new ideas.*'

What happened in the 1960s was too much of the willingness to accept things without question – a position ripe for exploitation by those who had the desire to do so. Indeed this is symptomatic of the whole of human history, but in the space age it was perhaps, and still is, more of an anomaly.

The predominant cult model in that decade, and one that lasted into the next two, was based on Eastern philosophy or, more accurately, a complete bastardisation of Hinduism and Buddhism – Hare Krishna and Transcendental Meditation being the most obvious examples. These were developed as kinds of easily digestible 'Mac-religions'. One cult group set up by the Bhagwan Shree Rajneesh owed its development to the hippy movement. In passing it is interesting to note that Stephen Knight, author of the flawed *The Brotherhood*, was a member of this cult for two years.

With a blend of Westernised, easy-to-understand cod philosophy and copious amounts of LSD these Eastern based cults became de rigueur on the Californian coast. In short they were an instant way for the new age Messiahs to make vast sums of money and at the very least exercise their fruity libidos and a suppressed will to power. Their followers, of course, surrender all their worldly possessions in exchange for vacuous guff about higher energies and auras. The 'ascended master' (or other similarly silly epithet) would then hang out with the Beatles, drive around in a gaudy Rolls Royce (or in some cases whole fleets of expensive cars), sporting tanned lovelies that dripped off every limb. Not once were they ever questioned by their acolytes as to why they were behaving counter to the *sacred teachings*.

Guru?

At the head of and controlling the 'groupthink' of the cult is a charismatic leader skilled in either psychological manipulation through a dynamic and hypnotic personality or the well honed, sometimes reckless use of bullying and physical force. In most if not all cases, the self-styled leader will make claims to be the New Messiah, Christ or his antithesis, Satan. Charles Manson pulled off the trick of convincing his followers that he was both.

Through the teachings of their loquacious leader the followers will reach the Promised Land, heaven or in the case of the Nazis, a Greater Germany. Some promise a rebirth onto an orbiting spacecraft where they will join a celestial brotherhood (not to be confused with the more extreme followers of *Star Trek*); others new-found occult powers and a winning way with the opposite sex. They all claim to be the true keepers of sacred and often ancient knowledge. Many are dropouts from society or refugees from one religion or another. Some are sexually repressed or the victims of abuse or at the very least a failed family and safe home environment. Of course some have come from comfortable backgrounds and have discovered the arts of manipulation to control others and are in it purely for the money or the power kick, for example Luc Jouret of the Solar Temple or Bhagwan Shree Rajneesh and his ideas of sex and meditation (can you do both at the same time?).

Cult Exiters

These are people who take on the role of rescuing people from the clutches of cults. Keep an eye out for these people in case they mistake your cabal for a cult. They are highly skilled in the techniques of de-programming individuals who have been 'brain washed'. Jane Campion's film *Holy Smoke* followed the activities of Harvey Keitel's cult exiter as he tried to extract Kate Winslet's character away from the group based in India, albeit in a darkly humorous way.

Cult exiters and anti-cult groups have and continue to play a role in monitoring the activities of numerous New Religious Movements (NRM) – the modern, less than combative term for a cult. In many respects they are just as guilty as promoting the idea that young people are being brainwashed by these organisations. The anti-cult groups have a tendency to create and fuel the hysteria and often fall victim to their own hype. Many anti-cult groups are Christian and therefore see the 'Devil' at work in every NRM as they do with cult's bigger brother, the secret society. When the authorities consult these groups on the right course of action the information supplied can be and often is misleading. That of course is not always the case. But as William Shaw states in *Spying in Guru Land*, the cult/anti-cult relationship becomes one of a dog chasing its own tail. Each feeds on the other, creating a 'looking glass world'.

The anti-cult groups are just as guilty of provoking a hostile reaction to cults as the cults themselves. In many respects most cults, on the whole, tend towards privacy whereas their antitheses wallow in fire and brimstone fueled hysteria, raging fervently that everyone is at risk.

Some cult exiters and those setting up anti-cult groups are often ex-cult members and have seen first hand the often nefarious and destructive activities of these woefully misguided cadres. This gives them a more realistic and controlled, hysterics-free insight with a genuine ability to help those desirous to leave the clutches of an NRM.

Cult-ure

Television programmes such as *Star Trek*, *The X-Files* and *Doctor Who* all develop a cult following. All six *Star Wars* films have done the same, but is there anything to worry about? Are children, and indeed adults, being manipulated by the makers of these programmes? Some critics would argue for the affirmative, but most see them as harmless entertainment. Certainly, many people do take their passion for such shows as *Star Trek* to excess and, indeed, it could be argued that they are being exploited by the vast array of 'merchandise' on offer – that they are trapped into believing a fantasy and turning it into a reality. Is the term 'cult' used on the game of football? No. But it is true that followers of the sport dress up in their favourite team colours, buy vast amounts of merchandise, paint their faces, analyse statistics, and claim they could do better than the referee, manager or the celebrity centre-forward and so on.

Both *Star Trek* fans and football fanatics (the latter being by far the biggest group in the world), all show symptoms of cult behaviour. In many respects football is a cult and people have died as a result of the game. Violence on and off the pitch is widespread. Fans who switch allegiance are ostracised from their community or pub and often clash with authority.

Ironically, those who prefer the world of TV fantasy never take a life and generally appear to be less unstable, despite the attitude of non-followers and the torch carrying taunt-ridden mob. No blood fuelled riots or deaths have occurred at *Star Trek* conventions. Both *Star Trek* and football lack charismatic leaders per se but maybe that position rests in the roles of actors or celebrity footballers with every word and pronouncement they utter being analysed, scrutinised and treated as 'gospel'. Like books in any religion the meanings behind storylines, words and character development are studied for special meaning. Football may lack this side but players are still treated like lesser gods. Obsession is common to all.

We may be too quick to dismiss 'cult behaviour' as symptomatic of the extreme outcast members of society when in fact it is an inherent part of the human condition. It is often asked in the media how people could fall for such and such a cult? The simple answer is because they are human.

Brainwashing?

The major weapon in the anti-cult arsenal is the use of the phrase 'brainwashing', a term that came to prominence in the 1950s. It was thought that captured American pilots in the Korean War were being brainwashed because on being released they showed sympathies for their captors' points of view. This is also known as *Stockholm Syndrome*. In a bank hold-up in Stockholm the captives, after six days with a lone gunman, felt more sympathy for him than they did with the authorities that had come to rescue them.

The term brainwashing was made famous by Richard Condon's book *The Manchurian Candidate* and by two films of the same name. It was a term invented by journalist Edward Hunter for his book *Brainwashing in Red China* but was nothing more than a concept born of classic Cold War paranoia but one that was not allowed to wither and die. The US military could not understand why American citizens had become sympathetic to their Chinese captors and the Communist ideology while undergoing debriefing back in the States. They assumed in misguided arrogance that the Chinese must have developed techniques of brainwashing. How else would an American become Communist? But it always happens. At least a few per cent of captured individuals become sympathetic to those who imprison them.

It is well known that brainwashing is a bogus concept. It simply does not work, but as a myth and, indeed, an urban legend, it readily serves the anti-cult movement, to those opposed to secret societies, as well as politicians and their ilk. There is a continuous claim that cults 'brainwash' their members into certain or special ways of thinking. Coercion and manipulation undoubtedly takes place but there is scant evidence for anything more powerful than that. Human vulnerability is perhaps the greatest weakness that can be exploited. The use of phrases, expressions and psychology all play their part and indeed these are employed to create a kind of group-think in which individuality is suppressed. But the most important aspect in cult membership is that the acolyte is willing to believe anything they are told. There is willingness to surrender perhaps, a deep urge to comply (for whatever social or psychological reason inherent in that individual's life).

There will be many groups or individuals who will accuse you of brainwashing your initiates so be on your guard for that psychological form of disinformation. See Dominic Streatfeild's *Brainwash: The Secret History of Mind Control*.

Parallels

Like the major religions they steal from, cults have ritualistic ceremonies. Sometimes there is a blood oath that the initiate has to swear or some ritual of renouncement as they pass from the unclean world of the profane to the sanctity of the cult. Here they also parallel the secret society as the old ways are given up and the new ones become the standards by which life is led in the new truths of the elite. The acolyte is reborn into a select enclave paralleling both religions and secret societies. Although to give credit where credit is due the major religions are, on the whole, open to all. If one wishes to give up being a Roman Catholic or convert to Judaism, one is not put to death. At least, not in the present era.

Religions themselves do not harbour secrets and their teachings are open to anyone who wishes to enquire about such matters, although they do tend to spout on about 'mysteries' where none really exist. Secret societies also share with cults the notions of secret knowledge and elitism; that the new adherent must never reveal the (always nonsensical) 'truth' kept within the walls of the cadre on pain of death should they expose said secrets.

Caveat: Should you choose to take the cult route be warned that it is a quick fix and nine times out of ten lacks the staying power of a secret society. Some argue there is no difference between cults, secret societies and religion and there is some truth to that. But who wants to be called a cult in this day and age? Cults tend to congregate on the lunatic fringe of human thinking. Remember though that Christianity started as a cult and look what has happened to that.

Some Famous Cults

Aetherius Society
Ant Hill Kids
Aum Shinro Kyo
Ayn Rand
Branch Davidians
Christian Scientists
Dianetics/Scientology

Four P Movement
Fountain of the World (WKFL)
Hare Krishna
Heaven's Gate
Kabbalah – Qabalah
Moonies
Mormons
Nazism
Order of the Solar Temple
Process Church
People's Temple (Jonestown)
School of Economic Science
Yahwehs

In Michael Shermer's *Why People Believe Weird Things* he lays down the basic characteristics of a cult. It is interesting to note that some governments often run along the same lines.

They are:

Veneration of the Leader: The leader is glorified beyond everything else.

Inerrancy of the Leader: S/He can do no wrong.

Omniscience of the Leader: Accepting without question everything the leader says.

Persuasive Techniques: The use of 'brainwashing' techniques.

Hidden Agendas: The real motives for the cult are kept secret even from adherents.

Deceit: The whims, failings, character flaws etc. of the leader and those of his or her inner circle are covered up.

Financial and/or Sexual Exploitation: Sex and money are the real motives for the cult.

Absolute Truth: That the leader is the only party to the real truth.

Absolute Morality: The cult has the only true views of right and wrong. Those who follow them are moral; outsiders and those who choose to leave are not.

These of course can be adapted for your secret society but if you do you may very well be branded a cult and have some cardigan-wearing worthy hound you in the press. Not something you really want as this is detrimental to your long-term goals.

> *Extreme and bizarre religious ideas are so commonplace in American history that it is difficult to speak of them as fringe at all…*

> Philip Jenkins
> *Mystics and Messiahs: Cults and New Religions in American History*

What's Needed for a Secret Society?

Here's your checklist. If you can claim as many of the following as possible you can safely say you have a secret society. Be honest with yourself though. Work on completing the list.

Claim secret knowledge

To be the true keepers of that knowledge and that it is the one paramount Truth

Claim long lineage

Persecuted by non-members, usually the Church

Accused of having hidden agendas

Elitist

Ceremonies of ritualistic death: passing from old life of the profane to the new life of enlightenment – a cross-cultural occurrence

Swear oaths of allegiance

Subject to conspiracy theories

Play on perceived power to induce fear and awe in the wider society

Threaten members with dire consequences if secrets are revealed

Sometimes have a charismatic leader or figurehead

The Pyramid of Power

Lunatic conspiracy theorists have devised a pyramid of power in which they claim to illustrate the hierarchy of control that exists to rule the world. The usual suspects are there but tantalisingly they leave the top spot, the pinnacle, blank as if to suggest there is a great secret power out there running the show. If pushed (not very firmly) the conspiracy theorist will instantly claim that international Jewry is the 'question mark', the real controlling force that runs all the other secret societies. It is of course a load of old barking anti-Semitic hysteria that has much in common with the theory that 12 feet high shell suit wearing lizards, with the power to morph into the Royal family (amongst other personalities), are running the world. Henry Ford's *International Jewry* and the more infamous and dangerous hoax *The Protocols of the Elders of Zion* with its '24 declarations' said much the same thing.

Selianinoff, a rabid right wing Russian journalist and Royalist writing at the turn of the 20th century, also got off on the anti-Semitism kick. He said that each level of masonry controlled the one below in a manipulative hierarchy but insisted that the masters at the top were (guess who?) the Jews.

A Selection of the More Famous Secret Societies

Contrary to popular belief the Lions, Roundtable, the Odd Fellows, WI, the United Order of Druids, R.A.O.B, the Shriners and the Rotarians have no desire to run the world (at least not yet).

'We roared with laughter...'

Michael Harding
Past President of the Weston
Super Mare Lions Club on hearing the
organisation was said to be part of a
Jewish conspiracy to rule the world

Freemasons

Everyone's favourite secret society and the first one that springs to mind whenever the subject is raised. We all know someone who is in the Freemasons but know little of what they do. For a long time they were top of the secret society charts but have slipped of late due to the resurgence of interest in the one size fits all secret society, the Knights Templar.

The Freemasons have been blamed (and continue to be so to this day) for all the world's ills, revolutions, wars and corruption. Behind every scam, shady political deals and business venture, it is claimed, there is a Freemason. If something nefarious is afoot in the world, guess who cops the blame?

In reality all that is secret about Freemasonry is the way in which they recognise each other. They claim a long heritage back to the building of the Temple of Solomon but the truth is they are a construct of the 18th century. They have not set their sights on world domination, whatever their detractors say. The name Freemason probably comes from the medieval masons who worked with 'free' stone, that is stone already prepared for building work and not the rough-hewn material.

The Knights Templar

Maligned and praised in equal measure. The Knights Templar is the uber-cadre of choice for conspiracy theorists and those who cobble together alternative histories of Europe. They were set up in the 12th century to protect pilgrims on the road to Jerusalem and as a result soon became fabulously wealthy. This, surprise-surprise, brought them into conflict with anyone who fancied having a pop at them out of jealousy – usually the Catholic Church. The Templars had a great deal of property and were in many respects the first international bankers. In terms of secrets anything goes with the Templars, simply because they kept themselves to themselves and generally kept shtum about what they were up to. This made it easier for trumped up accusations of heresy and Devil worship to be laid at their door shortly before it was kicked in by the heavy boot of the 'who's this then?' boys. It was said they worshipped 'Baphomet', which is either a corruption of Mohammed or is a secret Hebrew code word for Sophia, a figure found in Gnosticism. It is claimed they had a great secret as to the real nature of the Holy Grail. According to Umberto Eco in *Foucault's Pendulum* it was a laundry list.

The real reason for their demise is due to the enormous debt problem of Phillip IV of France who had them all arrested. He owed a great deal of money to the Templars and decided that the best way to get rid of his debts was to slaughter his creditors (modern banks should take note!). For 200 years or so they had gone about their business but all that ended on October 13 1307. By the early part of the 14th century they had been extinguished... or so we thought. It is claimed that they evolved into the Freemasons who have borrowed a number of ritualistic elements from them.

Knights Templar: Requirements for Membership

Poverty
Chastity
Obedience

Once initiated a Templar must swear to:

Never shave
Never surrender
Never offer a ransom if captured
Never flee a battle unless outnumbered three-to-one

Templars were also exempt from the rule and taxation of kings and bishops. For more, explore www.templarhistory.com.

The Illuminati

This is another favourite of the conspiracy theorists – usually those with an anti-Semitic stance. The Illuminati were first set up in 1776 (an auspicious year! – just a quick tease there for the conspiracy folks) by one Adam Weishaupt with the financial assistance of the house of Rothschild. It was based on the Muslim cult, Roshaniya. Both the Marquis de Sade and Francis Dashwood were part of the inner circle, which instantly alerted the pious to its supposed activities. The Illuminati were said to have infiltrated every other secret society, particularly the Freemasons, for control of the world's affairs. Some scholars state that they were set up to protect science and the new understanding of the workings of the cosmos.

In the modern construct of the Illuminati (it appears to exist only in fevered Internet imaginations), we have the embodiment of three primal Christian fears: Muslim cult, Jewish money and Satanism (as embodied by De Sade and Dashwood). The paranoid would have us believe that the Illuminati wish to rid the world of God, patriotism, nation states, monarchies and social order – all the favourites of the right wing! Gives you a clue as to who vigorously fans the flames of conspiracy that the Illuminated Ones continue to threaten society.

Opus Dei

A group with a distinctly fascist past that operates within the Roman Catholic Church. Of late they have been made more famous by the success of a certain novel. Opus Dei or 'God's Work' was set up by a Hitler-loving, liberal hating Spanish misogynist called Josemaria Escriva de Balaguer because he thought the Church was too soft on anyone who was not a Catholic.

Membership is by invitation only, much akin to Freemasonry, but that's where any similarity ends. Besides, Balaguer thought Freemasons were the work of the Devil. In many respects Opus Dei is an elitist cult with extreme conservative ideals and has been accused by ex-members of using 'brainwashing' and religious indoctrination techniques. Psychological control is used to keep members in check and is, in essence, built around a 'charismatic' leader who, despite his death, still receives personal letters.

In July 2006, the dismembered body of Gianmario Roveraro, a banker and member of Opus Dei, was found under a motorway bridge near Parma. He had been kidnapped two weeks earlier, leaving an Opus Dei meeting. Back in 2003 Roveraro had been questioned by the Italian authorities about the collapse of Parmalat. Make of this what you will...

Assassins

Once the fanatical wing of a Muslim sect called the Ismailis, the Assassins behaved however they wanted to because their teachings said that all action is morally ambivalent. They were founded in the middle of the 11th century by Hassan-ibn-Sabbah, a Shi'ite Muslim from Khorassan. It was not unheard of for Assassins to become friends with their intended victim and wait for years before killing them.

In many respects the Assassins were the blueprint for all secret societies that followed. Their system of grand masters, grand priors and levels of initiation were all nicked by the Templars and were hence handed on to the Freemasons et al.

Bohemian Grove

This is a summer camp where the rich and powerful elite of the United States hang out (in more ways than one, apparently). It is nothing more than a large-scale frat house for middle-aged men who should know better. Started in San Francisco in 1872 by journalists and writers so that they could comprehensively refresh themselves through late night drinking sessions, it soon began to grow in membership but with this came unwanted change. The wealthy turned up and changed the whole idea of what the Bohemians were about. Moving out of the city they headed off to the forests and developed pseudo-druidic rituals.

Many famous Americans have been members, or 'Grovers' as they are known: George Bush Snr, Walter

Cronkite, Ronald Reagan, Richard Nixon, Teddy Roosevelt, Charlton Heston, Dick Cheney and the conspiracy theorists' all time favourite, Henry Kissinger, who (according to the paranoid) belongs to nearly every secret society under the sun, so many in fact that it is a wonder he has time to do anything else!

It was once claimed that the Bohemian Grove was America's secret government. That idea of late, though, has begun to fizzle out but the Bohemian Grove Action Network maintain their vigil with the express desire of bringing down the Grovers. That seems odd in a country that prides itself on freedom. If the Grovers want to meet up, play dominoes and drink too much then surely that is up to them?

Hellfire Club

Set up by Francis Dashwood, who was sick of religion's hypocrisy, for his rich mates to carouse and blast their way through vast quantities of alcohol. He encouraged free-thinking but borrowed heavily from pagan ideas for his group. Because of this he was branded a Devil worshipper, as the term pagan then (as it is now) was synonymous with the Devil. Paganism has nothing to do with Satanism. Pagan originally simply meant 'country dweller'.

Dashwood had already set up a few groups in the past (Society of the Dilettanti, the Divan) but it was not until he kicked off the Hellfire Club that the fun really began. In 1746 he set up the Order of the Knights of St Francis who met in the George and Vulture pub in Cornhill, but he moved the group to a 12th-century Cistercian monastery called Medmenham Abbey near West Wycombe. He polished up the place with pagan symbols and redeveloped some nearby prehistoric caves (lots of lewd suggestive bushes near the entrance) to turn into the meeting place of his secret society. He also built a golden sphere with seats atop the spire of the Church of St Lawrence, modelling this feature on the golden sphere that decorates the Dogana di Mari in Venice.

There is more than a sense of tongue firmly in cheek with the Hellfire Club but then that was typical of the humour of Dashwood. When the sexually uptight, prudish and generally humourless Victorians visited the Abbey they set about ridding the place of its rude images. They were just another in the long line of those Dashwood was keen to wind up. Good man!

The Camorra

A secret society of southern Italy. Formed during the time of the Bourbon misgovernment in Naples, i.e. the early 19th century, and made up on the whole of the poorer criminal classes. It soon attracted the likes of the corrupt wealthy who under its banner could carry on their nefarious business practices such as extortion, smuggling and… well, you name it. Members were bound by a fierce and strict code of secrecy. Liborio Romano the last Bourbon minister of the interior, was heavily involved with the Camorra. After the union of the kingdom of the Two Sicilies (Naples) with Sardinia, Lamarmora, the Governor of Naples, pretty much squashed the outfit but it survived, evolving into a political party. Continued use of corruption forced the involvement of the Italian government of 1899–1901. Its name comes from the Italian for blouse – the Camorra – worn by the initiates.

Priory of Sion

Forget this lot. They are a bogus outfit. Pierre Plantard had a crack at setting up a secret society but failed on all levels. This is a great example of how not to do it and you should take special note to study the processes involved and why they went wrong. Nevertheless he had many fooled for a long time but made some grave errors along the way. Using the words 'Secret Dossier' on documents is a bit of a give away; at least a very bad tongue in cheek joke. A group once existed called the Priory of Sion but they died out nearly a millennia ago. This is a fine example of history being raided to add weight to a modern construct. All this did was earn a lot of people shed loads of money. It is a bit sad that their supposed best secret was that a mythical character was married.

The Ordines

This lot can trace their heritage to the early Renaissance but no specific date of inception is known. It is said they were organised to help protect burgeoning scientific inquiry from the inevitable onslaught of religion as important questions were raised about the world. Galileo's treatment by the

Church made certain individuals realise that the truth would not set men free but rather would simply result in them being burnt at the stake. Although Galileo was spared that fate he had to jolly well apologise for putting the sun at the centre of the solar system.

In later years a few conspiracy theorists have put them at the tip of the pyramid of power (a fabrication of the paranoid) to suggest that the world is in danger of losing any notion of god. Science is the enemy. Their motto translates as 'Liberty Through Scientific Knowledge'.

Other notable secret societies are the Rosicrucians, the Skull and Bones, the Charcoal Burners, the Garduna, the Holy Vehm, the Castrators of Russia (yes, they did!), the Decided Ones of Jupiter the Thunderer, the Bilderberg (jury's still out), the Knights of Malta and the Thugee.

American College Fraternities

Not as popular (in terms of membership) as they once were but they are nevertheless still an important part of college life in the United States. Phi Beta Kappa, the oldest fraternity, was formed in 1776 at William and Mary College, Williamsburg, Virginia and is connected today with the liberal arts. Numerous others exist in either the scholarly or business realms and there are more than 100 nationwide equating to 90 fraternities and 30 or so sororities. Beta Gamma Sigma is the most famous business one, while Sigma XI is for science.

In the past they had a more socially elitist feel to them with students either being called 'Greek' (superior) or 'Barb' (short for barbarian). In more recent times students have integrated more and have cast off the ideas surrounding the promotion of Protestant, Catholic or Jewish ideals for more liberal and inclusive activities. (See *National Lampoon's Animal House*, Dir: John Landis, 1978.)

Esteemed Company:
Inside the Freemasons

Some Famous Freemasons:

Buzz Aldrin★, John Jacob Astor, William 'Count' Basie, Irving Berlin, Mel Blanc, Ernest Borgnine, James Boswell, Robert Burns, Samuel L. Clemens (Mark Twain), Bill Clinton, Nat 'King' Cole, Cecil B. De Mille, Sir Arthur Conan Doyle, Edward VII, Edward VIII, Douglas Fairbanks, Gene Autry, Winston Churchill, William 'Buffalo Bill' Cody, Samuel Colt, Davy Crockett, Jack Dempsey, Valéry Giscard d'Estaing, W. C. Fields, Sir Alexander Fleming, Gerald Ford, Glenn Ford, Henry Ford, Benjamin Franklin, Frederick II ('The Great'), King of Prussia (1712–1786), Clark Gable, Garibaldi, George I, George VI, Edward Gibbon, Sir William S. Gilbert, John Glenn, D. W. Griffith, Virgil 'Gus' Grissom, Lionel Hampton, John Hancock, Warren Harding, Oliver Hardy, Haydn, Hogarth, Frank Hoover (of vacuum fame), J. Edgar Hoover, Harry Houdini (Ehrich Weiss), Burl Ives, Reverend Jesse Jackson, Edward Jenner, Al Jolson, Lyndon Johnson, Rudyard Kipling, Charles Lindburgh, General Douglas MacArthur, Louis B. Mayer, Franz Anton Mesmer,

★Now you know why some idiots think the Freemasons live on the moon.

Jacques Etienne Montgolfier, Mozart, Audie Murphy, James Naismith (invented basketball), Napoleon, Arnold Palmer, Pushkin, Ronald Reagan, Theodore Roosevelt, Richard B. Russell (US Senator and member of the Warren Commission investigating the assassination of President Kennedy, included for conspiracy fans), Felix Salten (creator of *Bambi*), Telly Savalas, Antoine Joseph Sax (of Saxophone fame), Scott of the Antarctic, Peter Sellers, Jean Sibelius, John Philip Sousa, Adlai Stevenson, Jonathan Swift, Harry S. Truman, Horace Walpole, Earl Warren, George Washington, John Wayne, William IV, William Wyler and Darryl F. Zanuck.

For a comprehensive list see www.masonicinfo.com.

Masonic Requirements for Membership:

A belief in a Supreme Being.

Being a man, freeborn, of good repute and well recommended.

Of lawful age.

Ability to support one's self and family.

Come to Freemasonry of their 'own free will and accord'.

Masonry Also Demands of a Candidate:

Sincerely desires the intellectual and moral improvement of himself and his fellow creatures, and that he is willing to devote part of his time, means and efforts to the promotion of brotherly love, relief and trust.

That he seeks no commercial, social nor pecuniary advantages.

That he is able to afford the necessary expenditure without injury to himself or connections.

That he is willing to enter into solemn obligations in the sight of his God.

Some Masonic Symbolic Images

The gavel
Chisel and maul
Euclid's 47th proposition
Pillars or columns, usually two, called Jachin and Boaz (representing *Forte* and *Sagresse* i.e. Strength and Wisdom)
All Seeing Eye
Square, level and compass (dividers)
The sun and moon
A chequered floor
Tracing boards
Plumb-rule
Stars

Five pointed star
Three-runged ladder
Globes
Rough and 'free' stone
Sprig of Acacia
Skull and Bones
Tears
Coffin

The Original Masonic Articles from the Old Constitutions:

Make careful note, there is nothing about taking over the world.

1. I am to admonish you to honour God in His holy Church that you use no heresy, schism and error.
2. To be true to our Sovereign Lord the King, his heirs and Successors.
3. You shall be true to your Fellowes and Brethren of the Science of Masonry, and to do unto them as you would be done unto.
4. You shall keep secret the obscure and intricate parts of the Science, not disclosing them to any but such as study and use the same.
5. You shall do your work truly and faithfully, endeavouring the profit and advantage of the owner of said work.
6. You shall call Masons your Fellows and Brethren,

without addition of "knaves" or other bad language.

7. You shall not take your neighbour's wife villainously, nor his daughter, nor his maid or his servant to use ungodly.

8. You shall not carnally lye with any woman that is belonging to the house where you are at table.

9. You shall truly pay your meat and drink, where you are at table.

10. You shall not undertake any Man's work, knowing yourself unable or unexpert to perform and effect the same.

11. You shall not take any work to do at excessive or unreasonable rates, to deceive the owner thereof.

12. You shall so take your work, that thereby you may live honestly, and pay your Fellows the wages as the Science doth recognise.

13. You shall not supplant any of your Fellows of their work altho' you perceive him or them unable to finish the same.

14. You shall not take any Apprentice to serve you in the said Science of Masonry under the term of seven years; nor any but of good and honest parentage.

15. You shall not take upon you to make any one Mason without the Privity of Consent of six, or five at least of your Fellows, and not but such as is Freeborn, and whose Parents live in good Fame and Name, and that have his right and perfect Limbs, and able of Body.

16. You shall not pay any of your Fellows more money than he or they have deserv'd.

17. You shall not slander any of your Fellows behind their backs.

18. You shall not, without very urgent Cause, answer your Fellow doggedly or ungodly, but as becomes a loving Brother.

19. You shall duly reverence your Fellows, that the Bond of Charity and mutual Love may continue.

20. You shall not (except in Christmas time) use any lawless Games, as Dice, Cards or such like.

21. You shall not frequent any Houses of Bawdery, or be a Pander to any of your Fellows.

22. You shall not go out to drink at Night, or if occasion happen that you must go, you shall not stay past Eight of the Clock.

23. You shall come to the Yearly Assembly, if you know where it is kept, being within Ten Miles of the Place of your Abode, submitting yourself to the Censure of your Fellows.

24. You shall not make any Mould, Square, or Rule to mould Stones withal, but such as are allowed by the Fraternity.

25. You shall set Strangers at Work, having Employment for them, at least a Fortnight, and pay them their wages truly, and if you want work for them, then you shall relieve them with money to defray their reasonable Charges to the next Lodge.

26. You shall truly attend your Work, and truly end the same, etc. All these Articles and Charge, which I have now read unto you, you shall well and truly observe, perform and keep to the best of your Power, and Knowledge, So help you God, and the true and Contents of this Book.

It is worth comparing these oaths with those of, for example, the Triads – see Fenton Bresler's *The Trail of the Triads* in which they are listed.

The Masonic Deity

Is Jahbulon:

Jah – *Jahweh* (Yahweh), a god of the Hebrews.

Bul – From *Baal*, the ancient Canaanite god of fertility.

On – From *Osiris*, ancient Egypt's god of the underworld.

Masonic Music

The Magic Flute by Mozart. One conspiracy theory has it that Mozart was murdered by the Freemasons for revealing secrets in this opera.

Getting Your Message Out…

The Internet

Generally, the Internet can be a useful tool but not when it comes to researching secret societies. Cyberspace is riddled with idiotic, hysterical, anti-Semitic, religio-paranoia posted by any evangelist bigot with an agenda. The keen enthusiast who wants to set up a secret society will soon realise that there are plenty of people out there who think the whole world is in some eternal hidden war between numerous cabals. The most persistent load of cobblers is that we are all under the thrall of one of these clandestine organisations.

Let them have their virtual fevered rants, then ignore it. It is all nonsense. It is to be avoided as a source of knowledge. Of course, once you appear on the Internet you will know that all your hard efforts have paid off. Someone is watching you!

That said, the Internet could also be a useful and, more importantly, readily accessible medium through which to transmit your ideals, methodology or conspiracy theory. To advertise your existence do not take the direct route, although you can do this of course. It is more thrilling to enter cyberspace in the form of rumours and urban legends. A web site pretending to blow the cover on your cabal can be an excellent way to promote your secret society. A web site that is created by yourself! Masquerading as someone with something to say about hidden agendas, you can inject your group into the collective consciousness of the public, playing on their fears in the process. It may be worth considering initiating a 'web master' into your secret society. The Internet is such a powerful construction it would be a shame to waste such a promotional avenue. Blogging is another idea to consider.

Pamphleteering

Last used, to little effect, by the Rosicrucians 300 years ago and not really recommended in this high-tech, silicon chip age in which we live. Handing out flyers in supermarkets and libraries is not really the thing for an up and coming secret society, at least not in this day and age. Nor, it should be said, is turning up on people's front doorsteps flogging your revolutionary wares. Nailing your manifesto to church doors or billposting them to the walls of your local town council may provoke some interest and is worth considering. This furtive activity should really be kept to the night hours. Be aware of CCTV cameras, although these too can be exploited for great paranoia inducing effect as long as you are dressed accordingly, perhaps in dark clothes but not regalia.

Literature?

You may actually decide that a novel is the best way to launch your secret society whether by your own hand or through the use of a commissioned ghostwriter. Normally it is wise to let others speculate with their own fantasies concerning clandestine cabals but despite earlier caveats it may be an idea worth considering.

Novels masquerading as history sell equally well as other works of fiction. If not a novel you might wish to create an historical 'faction' – fibs dressed up as fact. The usual elements of these kinds of works are hidden treasures, lost antiquities and revisionist history. Do not worry. You only need a little working knowledge in order to write these. What you really need is a semi-reasonable imagination. Do not be afraid to mix the themes for a really heady read. Work in a secret society or two, including yours, and you are home and dry.

Usual themes include:

> The 'real' meaning of the Pyramids of the Giza Plateau
> Cydonia and the '*Face*' on Mars (and its connection to the above)
> The whereabouts of the Ark of the Covenant
> The whereabouts and the true meaning of the Holy Grail
> The Turin Shroud as an ancient relic and not a fake^
> Alchemical secrets+

---

^It's a fake! Deal with it...

+Surely alchemy defeats its own purpose. If base metals are incessantly turned into gold, does that not mean the once precious metal eventually becomes worthless?

Ancient civilisations★ – usually '*drowned*' in a deluge
Ancient astronauts (see Easter Island myths, The Dogon
 in Mali, '*Landing strips*' in Peru, etc.)
Ancient megaliths as sources of 'mysterious' power
Atlantis
The Apocalypse
The Knights Templar and… whatever grabs your fancy
Ley Lines and landscape symbolism
Astrology and prophecy
The Bible Code $

The problem is that writing a book is a time consuming and often frustrating activity and having the work published is no easy task. Thousands of books are written every year and most are rejected and never see the light of day. Be prepared for a long drawn out process should you be willing to storm the battlements of the publishing world. It is worth it in the end though. Persistence is all!

★On one television programme about such a subject two individuals (one of them being a journalist turned cod pseudo-archaeologist), who should really know better, dredged up a stone with '*ancient markings*' on it. In reality those '*hieroglyphs*' were fossilised worm casts. Evidence enough to the fact you need no knowledge to produce such alternative views.

$Is Charles Darwin, DNA and Evolution in this code? No, didn't think so…

Real Power

Unable to control destinies on Earth openly because governments would resist, this mystic alliance can act only through secret societies. These, gradually created as the need for them arises, are divided into distinct groups, groups seemingly in opposition, sometimes advocating the most contradictory policies in religion, politics, economics, and literature; but they are all connected, all directed by the invisible centre that hides its power as it thus seeks to move all scepters of the earth.

J.M. Hoene-Wronski, quoted by P. Sedir,
Histoire des Rose-Croix, Bibliotheque des
Hermétistes, Paris, 1910

Now then, will you ever come to dominate the world? In a word, no. So put aside any romantic notions of ever doing so. The modern myth has it that this is a secular world – it is not! If anyone tells you that, they are a fibbing liar. There are perhaps a billion Muslims in the world, the same amount of Christians and perhaps that amount of Buddhists, Hindus and other sundry religions. The population of China must equal that amount as well. It is not an overstatement to say that over five billion people oppose you from the start. That is most of the inhabitants of planet Earth. As most of them believe in a deity of some description and have strict rules and regulations they are not going to allow you to run their lives (especially if you are leaning towards the liberal-atheist secret society). Never in a month of Sundays are you going to tell these people what to do. If you do attempt anything clandestine, a priest, journalist, revolutionary group, documentary crew, party official — the list is endless — will be on your back like a ton of bricks. It is simply not worth it in the end, so keep your activities (as Kennedy said) to the quiet work of centuries.

Note: Religions make great play of the supposed destructive influence of secret societies but it is a fact that more people have died from the result of religious ignorance and persecution than through any supposed dastardly plot devised by any secret society. More people are repressed, suppressed and maltreated by religious intolerance and extremism than from any machinations of so-called revolutionary, clandestine (usually liberal, atheist) cadres.

You could of course if you wish start your own religion but that is for another book and another time.

Useful Words

You may find that the use of the term 'secret society' becomes a shade tedious. Here is a selection of alternatives suggested by *Roget's Thesaurus*:

Alliance, band, body, cabal, cadre, cartel, clan, clique, club, company, community, confederacy, confederation, coterie, faction, fellowship, firm, friendly society, guild, house, joint concern, league, posse, phalanx, ring, set, sect, sodality, team, tong, trust, union.

Secret Societies in the Movies
(not including Satanic cults)

Keep your eyes open for more. Here are just a few to get you started...

The Skulls
The Skulls 2
From Hell
The Da Vinci Code
Secrets
Fraternity Row
National Treasure
Hour of the Pig

Some of the More Famous Secret, Semi-Secret, Benevolent and Charitable Societies

Ancient Order of Simps
Areoi
Assassins
Aviary
Bilderberg
B'nai B'rith
Bohemian Grove
Camorra
Castrators of Russia
Cathars
Charcoal Burners

Clan-na-Gael
Cult of Abramelin
Cult of the Black Mother
Cult of Mithra
Decembrists
The Decided Ones of Jupiter the Thunderer
Egbo
Fenians
Freemasons
The Garduna
The Gnostics
The Golden Dawn
The Hellfire Club
The High Priesthood of Thebes
Himalayan Masters
The Holy Vehm
Illuminati
Imandwa
John Birch Society
Kaioi
The Knights of Malta
The Knights of St Columba
The Knights Templar
Ku Klux Klan
Labi
Lions
The Loyal and Beneficent Order of Exalted Eagles
Mafia
Merchant Venturers
Minutemen

Molly Maguires
Odd Fellows
Ogboni
Opus Dei
The Order of the Peacock Angel
Ordines
Oro
OTO
Poro
P2
Priory of Sion
Pythagorean Brotherhood
Rosicrucians
Rotarians
Round Table
Royal Antediluvian Order of the Buffaloes
Shriners
Skull and Bones
Sons of Liberty
Sufis
Sukwe
Tamate
Tammany
Thugee
Triads
United Ancient Order of Druids
Women's Institute
Yakuza
Zangbeto

The SS must be treated as a secret society, at least at the very core of the organisation with its spiritual HQ at Wewelsburg Castle. Himmler imagined it to be a modern day group of pure blood (whatever that is) Teutonic Knights with initiation ceremonies and rites.

A Word on Secret Police

It is also worth mentioning the activities of secret police who often behave and act like secret societies. It is highly unlikely of course that your cadre will be asked to become a secret police force as these organisations are always created by the prevailing governmental power. The agenda of your secret society may of course be in direct opposition to the powers that be so this will automatically bar you from involvement. You may also be branded a vigilante group or a cabal with anarchic tendencies.

If your desires fit neatly into the activities of a government you may seek to recruit members of that ruling body to facilitate your progress and more importantly afford some protection during times of heated criticism. It is recommended that you approach that government's intelligence gathering community for recruitment drives.

You may wish to initiate members of secret police forces to keep them off your back, an action that is highly recommended. It would also be wise to seek out members of security agencies such as MI5, MI6, CIA, NSA, NKVD (aka the KGB), Tonton Macoutes, SS, Gestapo (careful research may unearth one or two surviving members) and the FBI, as these are very useful contacts to have. Having high-ranking initiates in powerful positions is always a rewarding and positive boon for your brotherhood. More importantly it can get you out of some sticky situations or if you prefer, into them.

A Few Places to Visit

The south west of France: the region around Rennes Le-Chateau and Carcassonne

The Hellfire Caves: West Wycombe, Buckinghamshire

Chartres Cathedral: see the amazing labyrinth on the floor

The Masonic Grand Lodge: Great Queen Street, London (you may have to sneak in)

Rosslyn Chapel: Roslin, just outside of Edinburgh

Ruins of the Mithra Temple: Temple Court, 11 Queen Victoria Street, London EC4

The old Golden Dawn 'Osiris' Temple: Bradford and Bingley Building Society, 37–40 Alexandra Parade, Weston Super Mare

Any settlement with 'Temple' in its name as this tells you that this place was once owned by the Templars, such as Temple Meads, Temple Cowley, Temple Cloud, Temple Guiting, Temple Dinsley and Templecombe.

Freemasons Hall

The present Freemasons Hall on Great Queen Street was built between the years 1927–33 as the administrative headquarters of the United Grand Lodge of England. It was initially known as the Masonic Peace Memorial dedicated to Freemasons who had died in World War One. The building was opened by the Duke of Connaught. There are offices on the ground floor, Grand Temple, library and the museum on the first, with various rooms on the second and third for various Masonic meetings, and rituals.

Great Queen street has seen three Masonic halls. The first was built in 1775–6 by Thomas Sandby of which nothing now remains. The second was built in 1864–9 and was designed by Francis Pepys Cockerell. Only a section of the façade of that building remains.

The End of the Beginning?

This is not the end. It is not even the beginning of the end. But it is perhaps, the end of the beginning.

Winston Churchill, 1942

Right, there you have it: the fundamentals on how to start your own secret society. Remember this is just the basics, from which to develop your own ideas, rules, regulations, initiation ceremonies and agendas. Remember, do not rush. Take your time and the thrilling results of your endeavours will be worth the long-term efforts. Disraeli said, '*The secret of success is constancy to purpose*,' so do not stumble over your own eagerness to get things going immediately. You will make mistakes but learn swiftly from them and be on your way.

GETTING YOUR MESSAGE OUT...

Critics who accuse secret societies fail to see that it is basic human nature that causes the problems. Greedy men are greedy men whether they are members of cabals, sects, golf clubs, mineral collecting associations or have no allegiances to fraternal brotherhoods at all. To accuse any secret society of a nefarious agenda because of a few bad apples is a nonsense. Remember, no Freemason brought us the Inquisition or a suicide bomb.

Wince Pewter
Why I Love Secret Societies

You will also come up against the fierce and strongly misguided opposition, part of the fun of course, but as Edmund Burke once said, '*He that wrestles with us strengthens our nerves and sharpens our skill. Our antagonist is our helper.*' Well said! The truth about your organisation will be distorted, corrupted and used as agit-prop for certain quarters of the establishment. You will be denigrated in documentaries, reviled by the right and left, 'exposed' in the press and accused of all kinds of heinous criminal activity. When this happens though, you will know that you have achieved that which you set out to do. Often a person's success is measured by the enemies they have – more successful, more antagonism. When that begins you will know that your secret society is in the ascendancy. You will have made it.

Most of all enjoy the experience!

And the best of luck! I hope to be reading about the conspiratorial activities of your secret society in the years to come.

There was a certain frisson on donning the apron.
I was doing that which was forbidden by many around me.
And I couldn't have cared less...

Peter St John 'Peeper' Dildee
28th GM of the Warning Boys★
Author of *Conform You Bastard, Conform!* 1952
And *It's a Secret, Stupid!* – *The Big Book*
of Masonic Humour, 1955

As the Freemasons say:

Happy have we met, happy we have been
Happy may we part, and happy we meet again.

★Not to be confused with the 18th-century Warning Carriers, messengers of the Worshipful Company of Goldsmiths.

Resources

Further Reading

The number of books related to secret societies now number in the tens of thousands. Freemasonry alone has generated at least 60,000 works on the subject. The following is a mere handful of recommendations.

Andrews, Richard and Schellenberger, Paul, *The Tomb of God*, Little Brown and Co, 1996

Anonymous, *Maconnerie Pratique,* 2 vols. Paris, 1885–86

Baigent, Michael and Leigh, Richard, *The Temple and the Lodge*, London: Jonathan Cape, 1989

Baigent, Michael, Leigh, Richard and Lincoln, Henry, *The Holy Blood and The Holy Grail*, London: Jonathan Cape, 1982

Baigent, Michael, Leigh, Richard and Lincoln, Henry, *The Messianic Legacy*, London: Jonathan Cape, 1986

Bartlett, W. B., *The Assassins: The Story of Islam's Medieval Secret Sect*, Stroud: Sutton Publishing, 2001

Bresler, Fenton, *The Trail of the Triads*, London: Weidenfeld and Nicolson, 1980

Brown, Dan, *The Da Vinci Code*, London: Bantam, 2003

Crowley, Aleister, *777 and Other Qabalistic Writings*, New York, Samuel Weiser, 1973

Dee, John, *Treatise of Rosie Crucian Secrets*, British Museum (An 18th-century forgery)

De Quincey, *Rosicrucians and Freemasons*

DaRaul, Arkon, *Secret Societies: A History*, New York: MJF Books, 1989

Dawkins, Richard, *Unweaving the Rainbow*, London: Allen Lane/Penguin Press, 1998

Eco, Umberto, *Foucault's Pendulum*, Secker and Warburg, 1989

Findel, *Collected works on Freemasonry*, 6 vols. Leip. 1882–85

Fort, *Antiquities of Freemasonry*, Phila. 1878

Gould, R. F., *History of Freemasonry*, 1886

Gould, R. F., *Concise History of Freemasonry*, 1904

The Handbuch der Freimaurerei, published as 2nd ed. of Lenning's *Encyklopadie der Freimaurerei,* 4 vols. 1863–79

Harding, Nick, *Secret Societies*, London: Pocket Essentials, 2005

How, J., *Freemasons Manual*, 1880

Howe, Ellic, *The Magicians of the Golden Dawn*, Red Wheel Reiser, 1978

Kaplan, David E., and Marshall, Andrew, *The Cult at the End of the World*, London: Hutchinson, 1996.

Kick, Russ (editor), *Everything You Know Is Wrong*, New York: The Disinformation Company, 2001

Kick, Russ (editor), *You Are Being Lied To*, New York: The Disinformation Company, 2002

Knight, Christopher and Lomas, Robert, *The Hiram Key*, London: Century, 1996

Knight, Stephen, *The Brotherhood*, London: Panther, 1983

Lane, Brian, *Killer Cults*, Headline, 1996

Leppard, Damian, *Fire and Blood – The True Story of David*

Koresh and the Waco Siege, London: Fourth Estate, 1993

Lyon, *Freemasonry in Scotland,* 1873

Mackay, A. G., *Encyclopedia of Freemasonry*, New York, 1874; new ed.1908

Mackay, A. G., *Lexicon of Freemasonry,* 7th Ed. 1885

Mackay, A. G., *History of Freemasonry*, 1898

Martin, Sean, *The Knights Templar*, London: Pocket Essentials, 2004

McCormick, Donald, *The Hellfire Club*, London: Jarrolds, 1958

Melton, J. Gordon, *The People's Temple and Jim Jones*, New York: Garland, 1990

Nicholson, Helen, *The Knights Hospitaller*, Boydell, 2001

Paton, *Freemasonry, its Symbolism and Religious Nature*, 1873

Piatigorsky, Alexander, *Who's Afraid of The Freemasons?*, London: The Harvill Press, 1997

Pick, Fred L., and Knight, G. Norman, *The Pocket History of Freemasonry*, Revised by Smyth, F, 7th Ed, London 1983

Pilger, John, *The New Rulers of the World*, London: Verso, 2002

Read, Piers Paul, *The Templars*, Weidenfeld and Nicholson, 1999

Riley-Smith, Jonathan, *The Knights of St John in Jerusalem and Cyprus 1050–1310*, Macmillan, 1967

Sagan, Carl, *The Demon Haunted World*, London: Headline, 1997

Sanderson, Meredith, *An Examination of Masonic Ritual,* 1923

Schauberg, *Vergleichendes Handbuch der Symbolik der Freimaurerei,* 3 vols. 1861–63

Semler, Solomon, *Impartial Collections for the History of the Rosicrucians*, Leip. 1768

Seward, Desmond, *The Monks of War: The Military Religious Orders*, London: Penguin Books, 1992

Shaw, William, *Spying in Guru Land*, London, Fourth Estate, 1994

Shea, Robert, and Anton Wilson, Robert, *The Illuminatus! Trilogy*, Constable and Robinson, 1998

Shermer, Michael, *Why People Believe Weird Things*, New York: Henry Holt and Co., 2002

Short, Martin, *Inside the Brotherhood*, London: Grafton, 1989

Sinclair, Andrew, *The Sword and the Grail*, London: Arrow, 1993

Streatfeild, Dominic, *Brainwash: The Secret History of Mind Control*, Hodder and Stoughton, 2006

Towers, Eric, *Dashwood: The Man and the Myth*, Wellington, Northamptonshire: Aquarian Press, 1986

Urban, William, *The Teutonic Knights: A Military History*, Greenhill Books, 2003

Waite, A. E., *The Secret Tradition in Freemasonry*, 1911

Waite, A. E., *The Real History of the Rosicrucians*, Lond. 1887

Ward, J. S. M., *The F.C.'s Handbook*, 1923

White, Michael, *Leonardo The First Scientist*, Abacus, 2000

Whitney, Edward A., *The Controllers: Secret Rulers of the World*, Rivercross Publishing, 2004

Wood, David, *Genisis: The First Book of Revelations,* Baton Wicks Publications, 1985

Yarker, 'The Arcane Schools', 1909, an article on *Illuminism* in the Edinburgh Review, July 1906

Yallop, David, *In God's Name,* London: Jonathan Cape, 1984